# AUTO REPAIR
# SHAMS
## AND
# SCAMS
## How to Avoid Getting Ripped Off

# AUTO REPAIR
# SHAMS
## AND
# SCAMS
## How to Avoid Getting Ripped Off

## by Chris Harold Stevenson

PRICE STERN SLOAN
Los Angeles

# DEDICATION

For George A. Stevenson, a best selling author in his own right.

Illustrations by Rick Penn-Kraus

Published by
Price Stern Sloan, Inc.
360 North La Cienega Boulevard
Los Angeles, California 90048
© 1990 Price Stern Sloan, Inc. Printed in U.S.A.

Notice: The information in this book is true and complete to the best of our knowledge. All recommendations on parts and procedures are made without any guarantees on the part of the author or Price Stern Sloan. Because the quality of parts, procedures and methods are beyond our control, author and publisher disclaim all liability incurred in connection with the use of this information.

Recognizing the importance of preserving that which has been written, Price Stern Sloan, Inc. has decided to print this book on acid-free paper, and will continue to print the majority of the books it publishes on acid-free paper.

**Library of Congress Cataloging-in-Publication Data**

Stevenson, Chris Harold, 1951—
    Auto repair shams & scams: how to avoid getting ripped off/Chris Stevenson.
      p.      cm.
    ISBN 0-89586-648-X
    1. Automobiles—Maintenance and repair. 2. Consumer education—United States.
I. Title. II. Title: Auto repair shams and scams.
TL152.S745 1990
629.28'722—dc20                        90-31177
                                         CIP

# ABOUT THE AUTHOR

Chris Stevenson is a former mechanic, with over 12 years of experience as a service manager, service writer, shop foreman, technician and journeyman mechanic. He has worked for dealerships, department store chains, quick-stop facilities and specialty repair shops. In years past, he has completed programs offered by the Allen Institute Training Program, the Toyota Service Training Program and he has been licensed by the California Bureau of Automotive Repair. Now a full-time writer, he is the author of *Garage Sale Mania* and resides in Huntington Beach, California.

# ACKNOWLEDGMENTS

I would like to express my personal gratitude to Mr. Duane Bilderback, Emission Control Engineer, Bureau of Automotive Repair, Sacramento, for his patience and opinions. He took the mystery out of the "Cat". . . Many thanks to Audrey Wolden and her exquisite editing abilities, without which I might have suffered all the typos, grammar errors and run-on sentences that I truly deserve. She is an author in her own right and I'm very proud to call her my friend. . . Thanks to Scott Virtes, publisher of Alpha Adventures, for letting me bend his ear, complain, nag and make a nuisance of myself. As a fellow writer, he knows how lonely the literary road can be. . . Thanks to Isaac Asimov for letting me in on a little secret called "The Unforgiving Minute". . . Much gratitude to Sharida Rizzuto of Baker Street Publications. She is a lesson in courageous behavior for all writers. When the chips are down, she shines like the Morning Star. . . To John, a very wise and honest mechanic, who taught me right from wrong, along with Gary Haskell and Jim Hill, at K-Mart Automotive. . . To my old crews at: Toyota, Mort Davis, Exxon, Shell, Texaco, Mazda, American Automotive, Goodyear, Econo Lube 'n' Tune and all the others. Much gratitude to Dave Russ, Public Relations Manager of the Goodyear Tire Division. . . Finally, thanks to my family: Mom, Jorlene, Art Post, Jamie (the cheek) and Mason (the short little mean man). And last of all, a thanks to my editor, Michael Lutfy, for making it all come together.

# FOREWORD

## BY RALPH NADER

Four out of five American households own one or more motor vehicles, and except for those who are home mechanics, most people must pay to have their vehicles repaired by someone else to keep them on the road. During the average length of vehicle ownership, the price tag for repairs could run into the thousands of dollars. Unfortunately, most of that money is paid to a commercial sector not known for its honesty and competence. How to find an honest auto repair facility in your community, and how to spot a questionable repair service or part, are the main objectives of this book, *Auto Repair Shams & Scams*, by former mechanic Chris Stevenson.

Before using this book, it is important to assess the need for its contents. A little effort devoted to understanding the following pages will save you time, money, irritation, anguish and the possible hazards of repair work not well done.

First the general problem. Just over 10 years ago, the U.S. Department of Transportation completed a study of the auto repair industry. Its main conclusion was:

"Approxmately 40 percent of the costs associated with auto repair are unnecessary. This translates into an annual consumer loss of $20 billion."

The Transportation Department study went on to list the major reasons for those losses as:

- Unneeded parts in package deals
- Unneeded repairs due to inadequate diagnosis
- Faulty repairs for which owners did not get their money back
- Unneeded repairs sold with possible fraudulent intent
- Unnecessary preventive maintenance
- Vehicle design requiring use of overly modularized parts
- Highly non-standard parts or excessively laborious repair techniques
- Accidents due to faulty repairs
- Wasted fuel

Today, the figure for these consumer losses has increased to approximately $40 billion a year. There is little evidence that the auto repair industry has cleaned up its act, or that consumers, the AAA or the insurance industry has organized to reduce auto repair fraud and incompetence during the last 10 years. To be sure, some state laws have been strengthened, most notably those in California. But the responsibility for curbing the rise in auto repair rip-offs is left to the consumer.

Back in the Seventies, another survey by the Department of Transportation concluded that almost one-half of the vehicle owners "lacked the rudimentary knowledge needed for correctly purchasing routine maintenance and repairs." Additional studies in eight states during the same period concluded that "40 percent of the auto repair shops charged for unnecessary repairs and 10 percent of them charged for work not performed." Unfortunately, despite these findings, little has been done to stop the fraud and deceit running rampant in the auto repair industry.

It would be useful to have more updated federal surveys, but due to the policies of the Reagan and Bush Administrations, the federal cop isn't always on the business-fraud beat. De-regulation has allowed the industry to operate unchecked, and the lack of federal surveys prevents the general public from being informed of any fraudulent practices. Consumers should be demanding monitored diagnostic inspections, better vehicle engineering standards, repair facility ratings and enforcement, similar to California's Bureau of Automotive Repair, on the state and local levels. Until that time comes, however, it is up to concerned consumers to minimize the risk of falling prey to auto repair rip-offs, and this is where Stevenson's book becomes invaluable.

This book is written for the layperson who knows nothing about cars. It actually operates on two levels—as a reference manual to be used as needed, and as a tool to help you deal with a mechanic or service manager much more effectively. As the author says, "with knowledge comes power, power that will make a mechanic or service manager think twice about pulling a scam." By understanding what should and shouldn't be done in the common areas of repair, and by understanding some of the technical jargon (see the glossary), you'll be able to keep a mechanic or a shop on its toes. The book's format does well in this respect, with checklists, cautions and sections on "scare tactics" throughout. I find Stevenson's description of repair managers and mechanics who "size up" their customers particularly motivating for motorists who see themselves as falling into a stereotype (i.e. family man, senior citizens, teenagers, women and single male professionals).

There is one subject I would like to elaborate on, and that is the use of the *Flat Rate Service Manual*. Though Stevenson does caution you to argue against these standard, pre-set rates and to question the length of time required for a certain type of repair, I don't believe he does so strongly enough. In my opinion, these manuals are rigged by industrial publishers to sell to repair facilities, who in turn will profit from the inflated hours listed in the manual. It is well to cast a skeptical eye toward any auto repair facility that determines your bill with such a self-serving device.

Hopefully, after perusing the contents of this book, you'll be indignant enough to organize or to join a corrective crusade with your local or state government officials and legislators in order to curb the fraudulent practices inherent in the auto repair industry. Wholesale justice is so much more effective than pursuing it on a one person, one repair facility basis.

At the very least, you'll be arming yourself with information about what happens to your car in the most common areas of repair, and learning the common scare tactics employed by mechanics to get you to pay for additional services and parts. This information is a perfect antidote for the mental blocks or the "take me, I'm yours" attitude. Though you may not know anything about cars mechanically, you'll soon develop reserves of self-confidence by using this book when the need for repair arises. All you have to do is simply believe that an ounce of mental prevention is worth a pound of dollar cure.

*Ralph Nader*
*Washington, D.C.*

# TABLE OF CONTENTS

# INTRODUCTION

The first job I had out of high school was with a local gas station. I was anxious to put some of the skills I had learned in auto shop to use, and was therefore eager to please my employer when he gave me my first real mechanical assignment after three months as a "rag wrench." Until that time, my job consisted of standing behind a working mechanic and assisting him like a nurse, swabbing his brow or cleaning his tools and parts. Now, I was finally going to apply the depth of my mechanical knowledge: to probe, diagnose, and fix a problem that had temporarily halted the operation of an automobile. Okay, so maybe that sounds a bit glorified, but at the time, that's kind of how I felt.

At the big moment, my employer asked me if I was aware there was a truck belonging to a paint company parked in back of the garage. I admitted I had seen it.

"Well," he told me, "pop the valve cover, tighten an exhaust valve, and then button it up."

I panicked and reviewed "the depth of my mechanical knowledge," because this didn't sound like any standard repair procedure that I had ever heard of, but then, who was I to argue? So I was convinced I was being tested, to put a system under fail, and observe its hampered condition so I could spot it later on when it actually did occur. It was an easy task and only took me about 15 minutes to accomplish.

Four hours later, the driver of the truck arrived. After he was given a running demonstration of his obviously stricken vehicle, the customer laughed and signed the repair order. His employer was paying for the repairs so all the customer cared about was when he could pick it up. When the customer left I was told to loosen the exhaust valve (tappet nut and screw), and adjust it back to its original position. I should then "plug it" (install six new spark plugs), clean the valve cover and head, then paint the works. I was to mask the parts very carefully and make sure that I used blue Ford engine paint. Now I was really confused, but nevertheless, I set to work.

As I finished up the job (which took about two hours), I became dismally aware that something was not according to automotive Hoyle. My suspicions were confirmed the following day when I took a peek at the repair order estimate for the truck and was astonished to see that it was written out as a complete valve job, including machine shop fees and other parts. The total came to $225! Minus my labor ($6.00), a can of paint, and six 40-cent spark plugs, my employer had managed to make quite a profit. But I was devastated. I had always thought mechanics were above that sort of thing. I was soon to learn that it was not an isolated instance. During the next nine months I counted at least 40 repair orders similar to that first one.

Years later I was working as a line mechanic in the auto repair center of a very large, reputable department store chain. While performing a standard drum brake job, I felt the heavy stare of the service manager over my shoulder. At that moment I was running a hone through the customer's used wheel cylinder with the intention of rebuilding it, a simple task that we were supposed to perform for free if possible.

"What are you doing Mr. Stevenson?" he asked. When I informed him, he turned red.

"We don't *rebuild* wheel cylinders," he warned, "We *sell* them. I want to see a new set on this car!"

I was therefore instructed to install four new wheel cylinders (this was a four-wheel drum brake car) at an additional cost of $23 each. Then I was to call the customer and advise him of this fact and tell him that he would need new "combi-kits" (those are the springs and keepers that hold the brake shoes to the backing plate) using the appropriate "scare tactic." By the time I was through, the advertised $49.99 brake job that caught the customer's eye in the morning paper now totaled $160!

The sham here was that the original wheel cylinders only needed a very minor repair and that our brake service contract stipulated refurbishing wheel cylinders if at all possible, a clause in the fine print we were to apparently ignore. After all, what were the chances the customer would inspect the wheel cylinders himself?

A great deal of my twelve years as a professional mechanic was in many ways rewarding, but I was often dismayed, and still am, by the everyday occurrence of deliberate and unfair repairs and charges made by mechanics in the trade. Speed, greed and the lack of informed customers have allowed many in the repair industry to charge as they like, do as they please, because they know that today's mobile society has you at their mercy. Besides, there is much at stake. There are an estimated 181 million cars registered in the U.S., and each year Americans spend nearly *70 billion dollars* to maintain and repair them. And no doubt, the feeling you had as you drove away after contributing to that tidy sum was something less than satisfaction of money well spent.

So what are you to do? Run out and take an automotive repair course and fix it yourself? Not a bad idea. Or arrive at the garage with a policeman at your side and introduce him as Uncle Fred? Possibilities to be sure, but not very practical. What you can do is arm yourself with enough information to deal with your mechanic or service manager more effectively. With knowledge comes power, power that will make a mechanic or service manager think twice about pulling a scam.

This book is a comprehensive guide designed to give you some of that information. I also suggest that you read over your owner's manual and consult a Chilton, Bentley or Haynes manual. Not so you can do the repairs yourself, but to familiarize yourself with the location and function of the various parts of your car. After all, you're driving a rather substantial investment, and are paying a lot of money to fix and maintain that investment, praying that it won't die at least until you've finished paying it off. So I would think that you would want to know there's more to your car or truck than just turning a key to make it go—especially if you can save some money.

I have worked for service stations, department stores, quick stops, tire and muffler shops, dealerships, distributors, and privately owned repair facilities, both foreign and domestic. The tactics used in each and every shop differ because policies differ, but the general consensus has always been to sell you as much as possible, with whatever means possible. Primarily, I will elaborate on the major components that are presently being oversold, why and to whom. I will discuss your attitude and posture to improve your ability to detect fraud and deception. Just exactly what does your car require every three, nine, twelve or twenty-four thousand miles? What constitutes a "tune-up" nowadays? What does it mean when a mechanic is "camping out" on your car? What's a "come-back," and why are there so many these days? If a mechanic tells you that your drums didn't "mic out," will you believe him without having seen them? Why does one turn of a screw warrant $25 extra on your smog check, because it is called a "low speed adjustment?" What are the typical qualifications for an average mechanic and why do they charge as much as your psychologist? Are you as angry as I am?

Good.

Then you'll want to read on, because if you have a driver's license, a pink slip and a set of car keys, sooner or later you're going to end up at a repair facility, whether you like it or not. You know it. I know it. And so does the mechanic.

# 1

# REPAIR FACILITIES

## CHOOSING THE BEST ONE

Before you can begin to choose where to take your car to be fixed, you need to have some idea as to what the problem is. Are you having trouble with the brakes? The front end? The electrical system? How about if the engine is running rough? To diagnose these problems yourself, turn to the appropriate chapters on these areas located elsewhere in the book.

Once you've determined the area of repair, the next question you're faced with is where to take it. Provided it's not a roadside emergency, where you are at the mercy of the nearest facility, there are an overwhelming number of choices. One flip through your Yellow Pages and you'll see what I mean. Which one should you go to? Should you go to the dealership, the department store, the big parts chain? How about one of those quick stops? Maybe you should go to a "specialist?" How do you choose?

That's a tough one to call. I can't make the choice for you, but I can give you a breakdown on each type of repair facility, how they are structured, and what types of repairs they are generally best for. I will also outline how most of these repair facilities charge for their parts and services. Why is this important? Because how a mechanic and service manager are paid often determines the extent of their honesty. If you were paid a certain percentage of every new part you were able to sell, what would you do? It's a good question, one that tests the morality of all mechanics paid on a "bonus & commission" scale. Some pass the test, many don't.

## THE DEPARTMENT STORE

I used to be mystified as to why the department store ever became involved in the auto repair industry in the first place. . . until I worked for one. After some experimentation, many department store chains have come to learn that certain types of convenient repair are highly profitable, and for the most part, can be fixed while a customer shops (and spends money) in the store. Most of the chains have narrowed down their services to areas that are profitable for them, and not beyond their area of technical expertise. Because of aggressive competition, and because of their volume, many a good deal can be found at the department store chain.

## THE GOOD DEAL

Though department stores will recommend and push parts with their name first because of higher profit margins, many offer quality name brands at bargain prices. The problem is you have to ask for them, otherwise you'll get their generic brand. Then again, be advised that most of the advertised specials they offer are only good if you use their parts, and not "the other guy's." You'll have to decide which is more important to you and your car—saving a few bucks or spending a few more.

In all fairness, however, many of the generic brands are quite good. A case in point is the Sears Die-Hard battery, arguably the best battery available anywhere.

Because of their size, department stores can offer tune-ups and brake specials that can save customers hundreds of dollars over some private repair shops. This is because they purchase in quantity, and their higher volume allows them to operate on a narrower profit margin than many specialty repair shops. That's the best case. There is another side to this as well.

## WHAT THEY DON'T DO

Most department stores don't handle any type of major engine overhaul. This would include valve jobs, timing chains, oil pumps, engine seals (front and rear main) and other internal components. Nor will they be eager to do any transmission work, flywheel or clutch replacement. Also rule out the department store for any type of electrical work.

All of these areas involve a vast amount of specific knowledge and specific parts for each type of car. The probability of a foul-up is greatly increased. Mistakes made with repairs on internal mechanisms are extremely costly, especially in the time/labor department. Also, many department stores refuse to work on "exotic" imports, such as Porsches, BMWs, Ferraris and Jaguars.

---

## CAUTION

*Department stores may not carry the long exhaust pipes and special mufflers for every type of car around, especially imports. What does this mean? It means they would often have to order the part from a dealer or special source—driving up the price of the part. Ask if they have your muffler in stock before you sign the repair order. For complete exhaust system replacement, a muffler shop would be the better choice since their parts availability is much better, although there are exceptions to this rule as well. For more on that, turn to chapter 5.*

---

## RATES

Some department stores have a "clock in, clock out" method of determining invoice and job prices. The mechanics simply punch a time card at the beginning of each job, then punch out. This is to determine the total labor time spent on the vehicle.

This method does foster honesty among the mechanics. Most repair jobs take about the same time in the hands of most mechanics. In this fashion the costs stay relatively uniform, and if a tire balance that normally takes 1 hour suddenly takes 3 hours, then something is wrong. How can you know what takes what time? Just ask the service manager when he writes up your ticket to see his flat rate manual, which lists the times for jobs. Then you'll have something to compare it to when you get the actual invoice.

With this system, the mechanics and service managers are usually paid a flat rate, without a commission on parts or extra labor. Therefore, these guys have nothing further to gain by overcharging you for their services or by overselling parts.

However, the majority of department stores operate on a commission bonus system, whereupon the mechanics earn extra money off of parts and services they sell above a certain quota. This method of payment can lead to dishonest practices.

# BEST FOR REPAIRS

Since we've discussed some areas the department stores shy away from, it is only fair to list the ones in which they excel, with a few cautions.

**Tires**—Department stores buy quality brand-name tires by the gross. Either that, or their own brand-name tires are manufactured by one of the big tire makers anyway. Ask the salesman who manufactures the tire for them. It could be the same tire as the one that costs $20 more, only with the store's name on it.

The inventory is voluminous and they stock tires for every make automobile and truck. They usually offer special, package deals that include free alignment, balance and installation with the purchase of new tires. Furthermore, the department store tire warranty is usually excellent.

---

## CAUTION

*Be forewarned that the extent of the tune-up may be limited (for what constitutes a minor or major tune-up, go to chapter 9). A department store's expertise when dealing with exotic or many foreign makes is questionable. High-performance foreign sports cars are likely to scramble the brain of a department store "R & R" mechanic. They seldom have the experience or technical repair manuals from which to perform the task. This is due to the new and sophisticated carburetor and fuel-injection systems and electronic engine control systems on many of today's newer cars.*

---

**Batteries**—Although the battery is definitely part of the electrical system, this is about as far as a department store will delve into this gray area. Most department store batteries are sold at very competitive prices. As with the tires, the warranty/guarantee furnished with batteries is outstanding and often includes an agreement to provide a trade-in exchange, which discounts the new battery price more. Courtesy inspections on these products are frequently performed at no cost to the customer. Costs on batteries vary with the type of warranty offered. Some are for life, some are for five years and some are for three years. If you drive a clunker destined for the junkyard within three years, or are going to trade in your used car for a new one soon, it wouldn't make much sense to purchase an expensive battery guaranteed for life, right?

**Exhaust**—Their exhaust work is thorough and they are quite capable of performing the work. There is nothing substandard about their pipes, mufflers, resonators, or hangers. However, according to a recent survey by a leading consumer magazine, department stores overshot their muffler and exhaust repair estimates by an average of 10 percent.

**Shocks & Front End**—Front-end parts are usually a bargain as long as the work involved is limited to simple items like shock absorbers. For more specific front end work, like bushings, anti-roll bars, springs, tie-rods, etc., you'd be wise to go elsewhere. For more on front end work, turn to chapter 7.

**Tune-Ups**—In general, most tune-up prices are grossly out of sight, but department stores are still a good bargain for a minor tune-up. Many of their coupon tune-up specials are the lowest in the industry. They do enough of them to be proficient and thorough, and they often have state-of-the-art equipment.

---

## CAUTION

*Don't get a coolant system flush and replacement from a department store unless they have a wall-mounted forward/back flush pump machine. You know you've been had if you catch the mechanic shoving a hose into your radiator and letting the water run. You could do as much at home. You need a good high-pressure forward and back flush which includes your car heater lines and reservoir—also a pressure check to see that your coolant system does not leak.*

---

**Transmissions**—A transmission service? Fine, as long as it's limited to a fluid change, new gasket and filter or cartridge replacement. It is a simple task similar to a routine oil change only it is for the transmission. Most of the stores stock the most popular service kits and the mechanics are skilled enough to provide this service. Insist on a good quality, major brand name fluid. Other than this, forget it. Most department stores are not qualified to disassemble and repair a sophisticated manual or automatic transmission. You're better off going to a specialty shop for this.

**Brakes**—Brakes are a major repair area for department stores. They stock nearly all of the brake shoes, brake pads and hanging hardware. Their prices for a two- or four-wheel service are very competitive and specials are always in evidence, usually run on a bi-weekly basis. Their best amenity for a standard brake job is low labor cost because they sell the service as a parts and labor package, instead of charging individually for parts and labor.

**Cooling System**—Department stores can do a great water pump swap. They do enough of them to be proficient, and their prices are nearly always better than a radiator shop's. Water pumps are relatively inexpensive compared to the labor charge required to install them. Hose and thermostat replacement are also very reasonable since most stores stock generic thermostats and radiator pressure caps. They carry bulk heater hose line on spools in all sizes, as well as pre-molded radiator hoses.

**The Little Stuff**—Windshield wipers, seal beams (headlights), taillight bulbs, inner tube and tire repair, fan belt replacement, oil changes and other smaller areas of knick-knack repair, are handled quite easily by department stores. Air conditioning evacuation and recharge is a common service provided by department stores and can be handled by most of the personnel, including the "general service" type mechanics.

## THE DEALERSHIP

For many years, the place most people automatically went to have their car fixed was right where they bought it—at the dealer. Not so anymore. Increased competition has taken away much of the dealership repair business, a business that represents a great deal of profit to these dealers. And they are fighting back with increased customer satisfaction training seminars, extended warranties and by offering you more "service" than you'd get anywhere else.

All dealership repair facilities are grand by any definition. The tools and machines are state-of-the-art. Their shops always seem cleaner and much more professional looking. They have elaborate parts houses, well-staffed coordinators, trained managers, paint and body shops, detailing crews, salespersons and beautiful lobbies where you can find color TVs, food and drink machines, classical music, polished floors and a cushy chair to recline in. The term "professionalism" rings loud and clear at the dealership. The image that they cast is just part of their overall strategy to cater to and to impress the repair customer. However, you will pay dearly for this grand show.

## RATES

There are few repair places where you will pay more for parts and labor than at the dealership, unless your problem is covered under warranty. The labor charges are high because the technicians are the most qualified in their respective specialty areas, and they are the most highly paid too. Because they are so familiar with your car, most dealerships use a flat rate manual that indicates a specific time allotted for a labor chore. If the book calls for 2.5 hours labor on a tune-up, and the shop labor charge is $70.00 per hour, the total labor charge (excluding the parts) will be $175.00. This leads to what is known as "flagging" time. A dealership technician is not paid on a bonus or commission scale. A tune-up can require 2.0 flag time, which means that it is a job that will take two hours (maximum), to complete. If his hourly rate is $16.00 per hour then he is entitled to $32.00 (these are his wages, not what the customer is charged.) This is regardless of how long it takes him. He could knock out the tune-up in 45 minutes (many of them do), but he is still entitled to his share of the full flag-time amount. You of course, are charged 2.0 hours of labor, even though the dealership technician may have only spent 45 minutes of that two hours working on that area. This is an outrageous system of charging that only profits the dealership.

**Parts**—The parts costs are high because they are exclusively "original factory equipment" replacement parts. If it is a foreign car dealer-

---

## CAUTION

*If it seems to take a long time to special order a specific part for your car that the dealership is out of stock on, then be sure to check the part number and invoice when you actually pick up your car. Occasionally, a dealership will obtain a lesser quality part if they cannot locate a factory original part. In this case, you should question the management and ask to see the parts inventory list on your invoice. The parts price difference between original and generic should not be the same. The generic should always be cheaper. The brand name is the giveaway. Ask them to itemize and explain each part number and brand name before you pay the invoice.*

ship, the parts are more expensive than domestic parts, because the long distance shipping and import tax charges must be offset. In most cases, parts at the dealership will be twice that of many other facilities. Every one of the dealership's parts is specifically designed to fit your car with precise tolerance, because it is a duplicate of the same part on your car, manufactured by the same people who made the car to begin with. It is almost never a reconditioned or rebuilt part, but a brand new one. That is one reason why dealership parts are so expensive. But think for a moment how necessary it is to have those exact parts. It may not be necessary for a muffler, or spark plugs, or oil and filters. Batteries, alternators, shocks, air cleaners, tires and wheels, brake pads and shoes—all are items that are available from other manufacturers that work just as well, and in many cases better, for far less the cost. On the other hand, if the items are fuel injection or carbureted parts, or any other internal engine components, then precise tolerance becomes important.

## BEST FOR REPAIRS

Most certainly you should *always* go to the dealer for any repair work that is, or should be, covered under warranty. If you go somewhere else to have that transmission repaired, the warranty could be void. The same goes for any heavy engine work.

---

### CAUTION

*If you're having any type of major work done to the engine or transmission, and your car is still relatively new, it may still be covered under the original manufacturer's warranty. Check the paperwork, then call the dealership facility and ask them if transmission or engine work is still covered. If it is, then you should go to the dealership. Not only should the repair be free (sometimes, however, warranties are limited to parts and you still pay the labor), but you should remember that many warranties are void if another facility other than the dealer performs repairs on warranty covered areas.*

---

**Major Engine Overhaul**—The dealership is a good bet for any type of major engine overhaul (internal work). There are other alternatives, such as specialty engine rebuilding shops that may be less expensive. Your choice depends on how much you value your car and how long you intend to keep it. You'll pay premium price for major engine work at a dealer, because the dealership uses all factory replacement parts. Technicians have all of the necessary current technical repair manuals and the latest tools and equipment to do the work. Any dealership parts house is superior in inventory to what a specialty shop might stock, hence the work would be completed more swiftly. Parts availability is crucial in major engine overhaul. The dealership excels in this area.

**Electrical**—Electrical problems can be the most difficult to diagnose in a vehicle, and dealerships generally are the best in this area. Most dealership technicians know the wiring diagram of your vehicle but even this area presents a challenge to the dealership diagnostician. Sometimes the short is interrelated with another system that has failed as a result of the original malfunction. Multiple electronic shorts are very hard to diagnose since no one rightly knows what system started the chain reaction in the first place. Finding a problem of this nature requires a slow, deliberate and intricate process of elimination. No other facility can remedy this type of problem faster or more efficiently than the dealership.

**Chassis & Drivetrain**—The dealership also excels in these two areas. This includes the major components of your chassis (all parts connected to the suspension, steering and wheels) and drivetrain like backing plates, driveshafts, differentials, transmissions, clutches, shock mounts, axle shafts, leaf and coil springs, steering components and other such parts. There is little the dealership can't handle in these areas. However, many of these items can be serviced by other outlets at better prices.

**Fuel Injection & Electronic Engine Control Systems**—Today's newer cars sport sophisticated electronic engine control systems and fuel injection systems that are exceptionally complex. In fact, the so-called "black box," the computer that monitors and manages your engine and fuel systems, still baffles many dealership technicians. When a problem is thought to be in this area, many technicians simply replace the engine computer rather than try to fix it, and send the suspect one back to the factory. The good news is that this item is almost always covered under warranty, so there should be little, if any charge for this service.

Sometimes fuel injection nozzles and sensors become damaged or clogged, and their replacement falls under the heading of critical work. In these cases, it is best to head for the dealer if your engine is not running as smoothly as it should. After all, if the dealership technician has trouble with these systems, how then can the local wrench at the corner gas station do any better?

# REPAIRS NOT RECOMMENDED

Can dealerships do oil changes, muffler work, smog checks, basic tune-ups, radiator work, tires and alignment and brakes? Of course they can, and with a great deal of proficiency and expertise. But in these cases, you might be paying for that proficiency and expertise when you don't need to. There are other outlets where these services can be performed at prices much more reasonable. Don't fall prey to the service writer's sales pitch that "we can take care of it now while you're here." This is an all too common ploy to help boost their profits, especially if you are coming in to have a problem fixed covered under warranty. A dealer doesn't make any money on a warranty repair, in fact he often *loses* money. So they are under a lot of pressure to get something out of you while you're having the problem fixed. Oil and lube changes, tire rotations, tune-ups, brakes, mufflers—are all areas you'll be pressured into taking care of while at the dealer. I wouldn't fall for them unless they are offered for free. These types of repairs are available from other outlets for much less.

## AUTOMOTIVE RETAIL CHAINS

These facilities include the major tire, muffler, transmission, and combination parts/service chains spread throughout the U.S. In recent years, they have become extremely aggressive and dealerships have watched their market share decrease steadily as customers flock to these centers to take advantage of their heavily advertised specials.

## ADVANTAGES

Many of these chains can offer highly discounted prices because they specialize in one area and do a great deal of volume. A tire store, for example, that only deals in tires with 300 franchises across the U.S., can certainly get a great discount on tires than someone who offers it as an additional service. The same can be said of a muffler shop. In the case of large parts chains that also offer repair service, their heavy volume allows them to offer replacement parts at very competitive prices.

## DISADVANTAGES

There are a couple of downsides to the larger chains. One is that they deal almost exclusively in *replacement parts*, which in some cases can mean inferior. Rebuilt and/or reconditioned parts are commonly used, and that is how the chain stores keep their prices down. This factor relates to just how much you value your car. I wouldn't want a Korean rebuilt water pump put on my BMW or Porsche.

Another disadvantage is that the personnel are often trained just to perform one particular function, like remove and replace tires or mufflers and nothing else. This is fine as long as that's all they do, but within the last few years, some of these specialty chains have begun offering other services faster than some of their employees have been trained to perform them thoroughly. A large muffler chain, one that built up a solid reputation for that area, recently branched out to brake service and shocks, high profit items to be sure. But I question the ability of the long-term mechanics who have, for years, only performed muffler work and are suddenly thrust into brake work. Brakes are not even remotely connected to muffler and exhaust removal and replacement. According to a survey by a leading consumer magazine, muffler chains scored lowest in customer satisfaction when it came to brake work.

Another factor influencing the level of competency are the salaries paid to chain mechanics. We're talking about entry level here. When a mechanic becomes extensively trained and certified, he's likely to move on, right? Therefore, I'm inclined to have a chain store perform only those services for which they are well known and respected for. Tires from a tire shop, mufflers from a muffler shop, transmissions from a transmission shop.

## RATES

Few people realize that many large chain stores, unlike the department stores, are "independently owned and operated" franchises. In other words, they are not regulated and monitored religiously like a department store service center is. Of course, the franchise owners are given policies and guidelines for charging according to a flat rate manual, but it is up to the franchise owner (and his service manager) to carry them out. The flat rate manual is really a form of price fixing. Quite often the time allotted is not how long it takes, but you are still charged accordingly.

Furthermore, this structure also usually means a system of "quotas" whereupon a franchise is expected to meet a specific quota each month. This can lead to overcharging and unnecessary repairs to meet those quotas. Unlike the department stores that used to charge a flat rate for the installation of a part (and some still do), chain stores for the most part have followed the dealership policy of an hourly labor charge. Chain store labor charges are usually higher than department store prices, but below that of the dealership. A few exceptions, like the largest chain stores, might approach the higher cost brackets, but they would still be below any dealership price.

## BEST FOR REPAIRS

Which chain is best for which type of repair depends on what they specialize in. Seems kind of obvious, doesn't it? The problem is, chain stores became daring very fast and began branching out into other

---

### CAUTION

*When it comes to generators, alternators, and starters, the main concern is whether the store stocks the proper replacement part, or must order out for it. Many chain stores do not have the stock rooms to house the hundreds of different alternators, generators, and starters for most cars, unless it is a parts chain (such as Pep Boys). So this "order out" part would cost slightly more. With these items you usually have a choice between a rebuilt or new one. If you do not specify which kind you want, there's a good chance the part will be new. The new part can cost 40% more on your invoice but the guarantee will be slightly better, for example, a 90 day guarantee verses the rebuilt guarantee of 30 days. It is entirely up to you as to which part will be used. If you desire the cheaper rebuilt version you must say so before the work is performed. (Many rebuilt electrical parts fail prematurely not long after installation). New electrical parts are less risky—they always outlast the rebuilt ones.*

---

areas. Many will repair (or claim to repair) all of the most popular "R & R" (remove and replace) auto parts and provide most of the light to medium type services. They will not, however, perform most heavy engine, transmission, or chassis work.

**Tire Stores**—The tire stores started out selling—what else? Tires and balance, then later, alignment. They are an excellent source for this service. They are unequaled when it comes to new rubber that is designed to last its maximum life expectancy. Their tire warranty/guarantees are the best in the world and, without question, backed to the hilt—satisfaction or your money back. Workmanship and tire quality? If it's a brand name, it's the best money can buy.

Since most chain stores (like department stores) sell tires, their primary product concern is selling new rubber and anything associated with it. As mentioned earlier, many of the shops enforce strict quotas on their staff to sell a certain number of tires per week. This is because they stock so many tires they must move vast amounts to keep their floor space free and ready for turnaround or restock. Therefore their prices are very competitive—the best overall buy in this product line. They also offer standard provisions for free rotation, puncture service and inspection. Many offer a "pro-rate" service that allows you to swap your old set of tires (if they have worn prematurely), with a new set of tires at a reduced or special rate. For tire quality, the tire chain stores are the best choice for price, quality and warranty/guarantee.

**Front End**—This is another area where the large chain store excels, especially if it is involved with the sale of tires. Worn front-end parts such as: tie rod ends, ball joints, upper/lower control arm bushings, shocks and wheel bearings can accelerate tire wear. Chain stores usually have mechanics trained well in this area who can perform these repairs swiftly and economically. However, unlike dealerships, they are unlikely to stock many of these parts, having to order out for them from a major parts house, or even a dealer. The parts mark-up may be high, but the labor will be less expensive than that of a dealership.

**Tune-Up**—Chain stores are well equipped to handle most standard and electronic tune-ups, with some exceptions (see sidebar page 15). Often their personnel are certified exclusively in this area, and they have the diagnostic scopes to perform them. Like the department stores, they run regular specials or coupon tune-up deals. The prices are hard to beat, besting the prices at department stores. The advantage here is that they will almost always use major brand tune-up components, and frequently there is a warranty that goes with the service.

**Brakes**—Brake service is still a good bargain at chain store outlets, in fact, it always has been. It is the one-shot price package that makes this service attractive. Dealerships or specialty shops rarely, if ever, announce coupon discounts for any type service. The chain stores know this and capitalize on it, by offering competitive, full-service brake specials.

**Electrical**—Chain stores can save you money when diagnosing common electrical problems with batteries, alternators, generators, regulators and starters.

**Muffler Chains**—Midas, Meineke and to a lesser extent, Ace, are examples of successful muffler store chains.

As far as work performed, and replacement parts for: mufflers, catalytic converters, resonators, tailpipes, exhaust pipes, exhaust manifolds, heat risers, hangers, (exhaust and tail pipe mounting brackets), the major chain muffler store is certainly proficient and well-equipped to perform these services. They will frequently run coupon specials on mufflers that beat the advertised specials of the department and chain stores, however, herein lies the greatest fault of a muffler chain. For more on that, turn to chapter 5.

## SERVICE STATIONS

This is where auto repair really started—the corner gas station. They were once the kings in their time and they harbored some of the wisest and most knowledgeable mechanics. However, the service station, which is usually independently owned and operated, has lost more of the repair market in recent years than any other facility. Many of them have shut down their "back room" repair facilities because they can not compete with the large chains and department stores. Many service stations that used to offer "on the spot repair" services now sell convenience and food items. However, some have held on to their repair facilities because they must have some sort of extra revenue—the profit margin on selling gasoline is so small. To compensate, corner service station prices are far higher than you'd find just about anywhere else. They can charge these high prices because the services they offer, either repair or food, are *convenient*.

Many service stations are family affairs owned and operated by father and son, cousin and nephew, or other relatives. The service station has always been the place where teenage boys got their first job. Generally, the staff is almost always limited, both in size, skill and technical expertise. There are, however, exceptions.

## RATES

Want a can of STP, oil, brake fluid or radiator coolant? No problem, as long as you're willing to pay as much as three to four hundred

> ## CAUTION
>
> *The fact that service stations stock little or no major parts means they have to order them or pick them up themselves. They might even pay retail for a part if they cannot locate it at a lesser price. This would lead to an already high priced part being bumped up more. Couple that with very high shop labor costs, and presto! You'll have a whopping bill.*

percent more than what the same brand-name items cost at a local auto parts store. I once bought a can of radiator stop leak at a service station for $5.95. Two days later I found the exact same product in a large parts store for $1.49. Simple mathematics is the greatest teacher in this example. Under no circumstances will I ever buy another product from a service station, unless I'm stranded. As for shop labor charge, the amount is somewhere between the chain store and the dealership (if it is posted at all.) This is invariably high considering that they might not have the greatest and most up-to-date repair equipment available. Their budgets do not allow them the amenity of the newest machines and test gear. An exception might be with a few of the largest service station outlets that are subsidized by the parent company, such as Unocal 76 stations and Arco MPG Tune-up franchises. However, the rates charged in a service station are generally as high as a center that has better trained personnel and better shop equipment. Lack of training and proper equipment could lead to longer labor times, which means more costly repairs and the added inconvenience of having to do without your car for a longer period of time.

## BEST FOR REPAIRS

They do quite well in most areas of simple auto repair such as fan belts, hoses, batteries, minor tune-ups and oil changes. Also, they have fared well in consumer surveys when it comes to customer satisfaction for muffler and brake repair work. In fact, they've fared better than larger chains specializing in those areas.

The problem is many service stations will tell the unsuspecting customer that they can repair *anything* for a price. You name it, they'll do it. Engine overhaul, carburetor rebuild, transmission work, clutches, air conditioning, electrical shorts, valve jobs—everything that a dealership could do these people will tell you they can do it, and for less.

They don't turn much work away. They can't afford to let you pass by. But I would seriously question the ability of a corner service station to rebuild an engine, or diagnose and solve a complicated electrical short.

What many of the shops will do, is sign you up for the work, then farm it out somewhere else and charge you accordingly. My advice is to stick to simple, remove and replace repair work when dealing with a service station.

**Emergency Parts & Service**—At night, far away from the big city, when you are broken down on some lonely stretch of highway, an open service station can be heaven-sent. In emergencies, most service stations are equipped to handle your problem.

They carry gas cans for rental, tow trucks for towing and jumper cables for starting. They generally carry fan belts and radiator hoses to meet any emergency for most vehicles since these commonly fail. Windshield wipers, seal beams and taillight bulbs are also in their inventory as are fuses. Other skills that they have related to convenience or emergency care are with water pumps, cooling, vacuum and air conditioning hose service. Their air conditioning service might be less expensive than a department store would charge as it is a very frequent service requested of them, especially from vacationers. They stock headlamp bulbs for most cars. Sometimes, a service station is the only facility around that will repair your flat tire and provide instructions or repair on tow bars, trailer hitches, taillight wiring and snow chains.

However, many a service station has been known to take advantage of the tourist stranded out in the middle of nowhere. "60 Minutes" placed a hidden camera at several remote service stations and recorded some very unethical and shady practices. Spilling oil under a customer's car, for instance, to sell a shock absorber or an oil pan gasket, is one.

In fact, the number one reason most people go to a service station for repair is because they have no other choice, and there are many crooked service station people who know this. When you've broken down on the road, a service station is the first place you're likely to be towed. Once the station owner knows you're stuck, from out of town and in a hurry, watch out! With a shady owner, it's rip-off time!

**Official Repairs & Services**—Most popular service stations post large blue signs that denote official or certified special services. Among these are: "Official Brake Station," "Official Head Lamp Adjusting Station" and "Official Smog Check Station." These signs mean that there is at least one person who has passed an exam and received a certificate or license designating that he can perform these repairs accurately. Prices for these services are generally competitive because they are subject to a "fixed" rate within the industry, or at least they should be. If you go to a service station for an official service, look for the state licenses that should be on display to make sure the station is qualified to perform the service.

# THE QUICK STOPS

The food industry no longer has a monopoly on fast service anymore. The concept has reared its capitalistic head in the auto repair industry. The newest phenomenon has been the concept of the fast repair shop, or the one-stop in-and-out service visit. Thousands of these small franchise outlets have popped up all over the U.S. Some of them are refurbished service stations. All claim that they can perform a simple service "while you wait" in about the same time it takes for a full-service car wash. Such a deal.

To a certain extent, the deal is pretty good. The only thing that distresses me about these small service centers is how fast they work. If you observe the work while you wait, you'll see what I mean. Several mechanics literally rush about your car in a frenzy to complete that "23-point" service to get it as done as fast as possible. These places depend on high turnover and volume for survival, and your service will be delivered accordingly. In other words, this type of work philosophy breeds carelessness and mistakes, which can become costly to you.

Take an oil change, for instance. In his rush to get it done, it is quite conceivable that a mechanic could forget to tighten that oil filter, cap or oil pan bolt securely, or forget to fill it up properly. You drive down the road, and suddenly your oil light comes on as the engine loses oil pressure, which results in a muffled explosion and a lot of blue smoke. What you have now is a blown engine that resulted from a carelessly tightened oil pan bolt.

## RATES

The rates charged at the quick stops are extremely competitive and relatively low, which makes them an attractive alternative. They are generally based on a "package" deal that includes fluid checks, parts and labor, all for a single low price. However, anything that falls outside the package, such as additional labor, an unspecified part, or additional fluids, are charged at a premium. They mimic the cut-rate specials of the popular chain stores to stay competitive, but on the other hand they charge very high shop labor costs appearing to mirror the image of a professional dealership.

## BEST FOR REPAIRS

These facilities like to concentrate in three areas, and generally do not venture outside them. They don't have the large stockrooms or trained personnel to service cars that require large parts, i.e. mufflers brakes, front end parts, etc. What's hot on their list are; lube oil and filter, tune-ups, transmission fluid change and (in California) smog checks. In fact, if such a facility offered to repair anything but what they advertised, I would thank them very much and leave.

**Tune-Ups & Smog Checks**—These shops do a tremendous number of tune-ups and smog inspections. Customers flock to the specials both for the price and the promise of speedy work. They probably know how to tune-up many import cars, and yes, swiftly—again because it is this "flea market" mentality that gives them such a good customer draw. Since a smog check and certification is such a dreaded inconvenience, most people want this service done quickly and out of the way. The temptation to drive in and drive out of such a small, convenient facility is what has given the quick stops so much smog check business. But a good, thorough L.O.F. should take more than 10 minutes. Likewise for a smog check. However, if you're in a hurry (who isn't in today's work work work society), then this minor fault can be easily rationalized.

**Fluid Changes**—The quick stops probably do more lube, oil and filter work than any other repair facility on an employee-to-workload ratio. It is their most frequent repair request. Transmission service (fluid and filter change) is another service offered. If they are a busy shop they perform many of these a day, and with repetition comes experience and expertise, but so does boredom and carelessness.

---

## CAUTION

*I would make sure that their replacement parts (tune-up kits, spark plugs, wires) are not substandard. Recognizable names are: Champion, Autolite, Delco Remy, Motorcraft, etc. Furthermore, you should be aware that a $49.95 tune-up constitutes a* minor, *not* major *tune-up. For the differences between the two, go to chapter 9.*

---

Be advised though that many advertise a multi-step service for a flat fee, such as "change oil, filter, check washer fluid, check coolant level, check transmission fluid, etc." The point here to remember is the word "check." If the transmission fluid is low after they've checked it, they will fill it, but charge you extra for the fluid. It is not part of the package price. The same goes for the other fluids as well. I know of more than one person who has been surprised by a bill far more than the advertised price because these fluids were "checked" all right, but then the charge to fill them was added on. I would advise that you ask up front what the advertised price includes.

## PRIVATE SPECIALTY SHOPS

As a result of increased competition and the need to specialize, the specialty shop has found a rewarding place for itself in the auto repair industry. Since the advent of the computer—the electronic control module, or ECM, more technical knowledge is needed to repair and diagnose the latest models. Systems like anti-lock brake systems, computer controlled heating and air conditioning, and computer controlled fuel delivery systems have created more opportunities on the car to cause difficulty. These subsystems are becoming extremely difficult to repair without special training.

Dealership repair and parts houses are finding it very difficult to hang on to faithful service customers, who are only revisiting the dealership for annoying warranty work instead of returning for routine maintenance, avoiding high priced general service altogether in favor of the less expensive chains and department stores. Only the chains and department stores are generally baffled by these new computer controlled systems and faced with the choice of trying to fix it, or send it off down the road to another facility. That's where the specialty shop comes in.

The specialty shops evolved as an "intermediary," providing quality repair without the high dealership prices. Nowhere has this service been needed more than in the foreign automotive repair trade.

Specialty shops are easily recognized by their titles or repair claims. For instance, shops who specialize will work on only one, two, or sometimes three specific make foreign automobiles like: Toyota, Honda, Volkswagen, Saab, Renault, Nissan and Audi, or any combination. By repairing only one or two models, the specialty shops can almost insure total working expertise in all repair areas. Specialty tools, testing gear, and other equipment are available. Customer satisfaction and speedy repairs (with less errors) are enhanced. At the same time overhead for the specialty shops is kept to a minimum as their rents and staff are kept down to provide functional shops that are half the size of standard dealerships. And best of all, the specialty shops nearly always undercut the labor and parts costs of the dealership. More than likely, the owners and operators of specialty auto repair are displaced dealership technicians and service managers who have branched out on their own.

## RATES

Specialty shops nearly always undercut the dealership price or offer other services at reduced savings. However, their prices will be higher than all of the other facilities: chain stores, department stores, gas stations, quick stops, etc. With this price you can expect quality workmanship rivaling that of the parent dealership, perhaps surpassing it in some areas. Furthermore, a specialist, trained to work on a single make vehicle, is more likely to be more familiar with that type car and repair it much more quickly than other types of mechanics.

## BEST FOR REPAIRS

There isn't too much that has to be said about the areas in which specialty shops excel. The term "dealership quality" says it all. If you own a Toyota, for instance, there is a good chance that the specialty shop will be able to repair any system on it no matter what the ailment. However, I wouldn't have a specialty shop change the oil, but I would certainly have them perform a major tune-up or solve an electrical problem.

---

### HINT

*When searching for a repair facility, check to see if it is approved by the AAA. If it is, this would weigh heavily in your favor, because the facility must adhere to certain requirements to get this approval. You don't have to be a member of the AAA to use the facility.*

*In order to receive the AAA seal of approval, the facility must offer a 90-day or 4,000 mile guarantee on parts and labor. Second, they must make available to you any parts that were replaced. Third, if the repair looks like it will exceed the original estimate by 10%, they must get your authorization. And last, the facility must agree to cooperate with AAA in investigating and resolving any disputes between the facility and an AAA member, and abide by the AAA's decision.*

---

## CALL FIRST

When choosing a repair facility, I highly recommend that you call ahead first and ask several questions. I do not recommend that you try to describe the problem over the phone, because most repair places simply cannot tell you what is wrong in this manner. Get a note pad to jot down the responses of each repair facility. When you've called around, compare the notes before calling one back and setting up an appointment. See the checklist for suggested questions you should ask.

✔ Call ahead and ask the facility if they have experience working on your type of car (unless it's a listed specialist or dealer, of course).

✔ Determine if the facility is capable of performing the work, if you know what area the problem is in. Do they do brakes? Do they do transmission work? If yes, what special certification do they have?

---

✔ Does the facility do their own machine work, such as brake turning, or do they farm that work out to other shops?

✔ Is the facility (in California) a member of the Bureau of Automotive Repair? Are their mechanics NIASE certified? If not, how are they certified? Is the facility approved by the AAA?

✔ If you're calling about an advertised special, ask what the price includes. Does it include labor, all parts, diagnosing and machine work?

✔ Does the facility give free estimates? Do they charge for troubleshooting and diagnosing problems?

✔ Does the facility offer a warranty on all parts and labor? If so, how is it limited and how long is it good for?

✔ Do they stock the parts you'll need? Are the items new, used or rebuilt/reconditioned? If they don't stock them, where do they get them?

✔ If you're looking for a tune-up, ask the facility what they consider to be the difference between a major and a minor tune-up. What does each include? How much is each one? What kind of diagnostic machinery do they have to perform it?

✔ If the procedure is a standard remove & replace job, ask how much time they generally estimate to complete the actual repair, and how long you'll have to leave your car to get the job done. A warning flag should go up if one facility says it needs 3 hours to do a tune-up and the other needs only 1 hour. Which one do you think will be cheaper?

✔ If it's a tire store, ask what the purchase price of tires includes. What kind of guarantee/warranty? Does the price include a free spin balance and wheel alignment? If not, how much do these necessary services cost?

# 2

# THE MECHANICS

## WHO ARE THESE GUYS AND HOW ARE THEY TRAINED?

Now that you've determined that you have a problem, and narrowed down the choice of repair facilities, you should be briefed on the background of the people you'll be dealing with. Years ago, a mechanic was a guy who was good with his hands who fixed cars. Not any more. In fact, with the complexity of today's machines, the technical knowledge that these guys must possess is staggering, especially dealership "technicians." There are over 420,000 pages of Ford service manual material that a Ford dealership technician should be familiar with. Does he know them all? No. Is he required to know them all? Again, no. And with the cars segueing into computers each year, the problem of finding qualified mechanics will continue to escalate. It is estimated that by the year 2000 there will be a shortage of 90,000 qualified automotive mechanics, which means there will most likely be a plethora of unqualified mechanics out there who say they can fix your car as long as you pay cash. It also means that more training will be required, more licenses, seminars and who knows? It may get to the point where a degree in engineering is required to work on the cars of the near future.

Currently, there are some checks and balances, as well as certificates, that you can ask to see to make sure that the mechanic you choose is somewhat qualified.

## THE EVOLUTION OF THE MECHANIC

Back in the early days, when the automobile first began to transform society, most people thought of the mechanic as a sort of wizard. He possessed a secret working knowledge about the horseless buggies that fascinated and confused most owners, who only cared that it went from point A to point B. When the darn thing stopped running, the mechanic reached into his magic bag of tricks to make it work again. It didn't matter how he got it back on the road. The fact remained that he did it and with apparent ease—a trick, a secret—something that was akin to turning base metal into gold.

The truth of the matter was, most of the mechanics of yesteryear had learned from the school of hard knocks, skinned knuckles and bashed fingers, as well as plenty of trial-and-error. If the domestic manufacturers did not supply an adequate repair manual (most of them didn't), or if the mechanic did not have one to refer to (he usually didn't), the odds were that he would dismantle three times as many parts as he had to to get the job done. Even this was not fail-safe since he always ran the risk of forgetting the assembly order of the pile of parts that now lay scattered about his shop.

In the decades that followed, cars became larger, heavier and more elaborate in design. They evolved into more than just a vehicle for transportation, transforming into a status symbol and a small extension of the home, equipped with as many creature comforts the chassis could withstand; heaters, air conditioners, radios, electric seats, automatic windshield washers, turn signals and anything else that could be dreamed up were added. But added comfort and convenience could also translate into headaches and more trips to the repair shop. Put simply, there were now more things that could go wrong.

## CERTIFICATION & LICENSES

How are mechanics trained and certified? How and where do they get their licenses? What organizations exist that are responsible for training and certification? Why are nearly all of the training programs voluntary? With the lofty hourly repair rates being charged, are you sure that you are receiving these services by skilled and certified professionals, or, is the fact that all mechanics are licensed and certified, illusionary? These are just a few of the questions we must ask. In no other industry will you find such a blurred line of distinction between those who are really qualified and those who are not. Let's examine some organizations who are presently implementing training and certification programs.

**NIASE**—This is the abbreviation for the National Institute for Automotive Service Excellence. This independent, non-profit organization has been testing the competence of automotive mechanics since 1972. NIASE is governed by a Board of Directors that represents all sectors of the automotive industry, as well as the educational community, government and consumer groups. NIASE's primary function is to test and certify automobile and heavy-duty truck technicians, body repairers and painters. Their program consists of a series of written tests given twice yearly in over 400 locations throughout the country. When a technician passes one or more tests, and has completed the required two years of related work experience, he is officially certified; given a "blue seal" patch, certificate, and pocket credentials. The questions are written by a panel of technical service experts from domestic and import vehicle manufacturers, repair and test equipment and parts manufacturers, plus vocational educators.

NIASE tests in the following areas: Engine Repair, Engine Performance, Suspension and Steering, Brakes, Automatic Transmission/Transaxle, Manual Drivetrain and Axles, Electrical Systems, and Heating and Air Conditioning. *However, the technician need pass only one test in one repair area to be certified.* So don't assume that if a mechanic shows you his NIASE card that he is qualified to work on any area of the car, unless the patch or certificate says, "Master Automobile Technician," which signifies he has passed all eight areas.

NIASE certifications are valid for 2 years, after which time technicians must recertify to keep up with changing technology. The NIASE testing and certification program is the largest and most recognized in the country. Most of these certified technicians can be found in dealerships, and shops who prefer their technicians certified. Since certification is not strictly enforced, the certifications are wide-spread, and not any one repair facility employs NIASE certified staff exclusively, unless it is their decision to do so. Currently, there are over 200,000 NIASE certified technicians in the U.S. Let's hope you find one.

**The Bureau**—The Bureau Of Automotive Repair (BAR) is an agency that is part of the California Department of Consumer Affairs, and it is responsible for the licensing of qualified inspection/repair technicians for the purpose of smog, headlamp and brake certification. *Test-only* mechanics are permitted to test and inspect vehicles according to BAR procedures. Qualified test-only mechanics are prohibited, by definition, from doing vehicle repairs or from conducting after-repair certification tests. Qualified *test/repair* mechanics may conduct both initial and after-repair certification tests as well as vehicle emission control system adjustments and repairs to failed vehicles.

Mechanic applicants for either test or test/repair qualification must submit an application with a nominal fee to the BAR office. They then must prove successful completion of the Bureau's "Clean Air Car Course" (smog), from an institution recognized by the bureau. Such educational institutions, like the *Allen Training Facility*, have courses which last 54 hours and cover all aspects of emission control related work and study preparation. A proficiency exam is required by the educating institute, as is an additional exam served by the BAR office given at a later date. Both exams are similar to the NIASE tests, including multiple and true/false questions, except that they are related to the most popular sought after license—the smog test/repair license. The qualification license expires in two years and the applicant must reregister and take another exam to be awarded a new license.

The owner or manager of a repair facility can be a licensed Inspector by sending in an application fee and a signed declaration. The declaration states that he is the operator of the station and is responsible for the validity of the tests, repairs and compliance with Bureau-prescribed Inspection and/or repair procedures. He is also responsible for the receipt, handling, exchanging and immediate forwarding of cassette tapes (shop records) to the state. An Inspector need not be a test/repair mechanic, but he cannot perform any smog check inspections or repair unless he is a licensed test/repair mechanic. An Inspector's license expires in one year. Both the test/repair mechanic or Inspector whose license has expired cannot perform any relative tests or repairs for which they have been previously licensed by the BAR.

The guidelines set forth by the BAR are specific and unbending. Any mechanic who wants to perform smog checks or other certifications must abide by the standards and practices of the BAR and the pursuant sections as ascribed by the California state vehicle code. Any shop or repair station that displays official certification emblems or signs indicates to the public that there is a BAR licensed test/repair mechanic and/or inspector on the premises at all times. Smog licensed mechanics and inspectors are required to display these licenses in plain view on the shop premises.

Unfortunately, California is the only state that has such a regulatory agency. Hopefully, other states will institute similar programs soon.

**In-House Certification**—Many automobile manufacturers sponsor their own testing and certification programs. One such example is *Toyota's Technical Training* facility in California, which serves the needs of distributors and dealerships. These testing and certification programs are aimed at the technicians who work specifically with a certain make automobile. The programs include update seminars on new models, along with problem solving classes in certain areas of diagnosis and repair. The very nature of these testing and certification programs limits the technicians to work and study only on the manufacturers models. Courses of study and certification include pre-delivery service and optional equipment installation, which make up a large part of the programs.

Through cooperating colleges and technical schools around the country, GM, Ford and Chrysler offer two-year programs leading to an Associate Degree in Automotive Technology. The training is comparatively better with these larger programs, combining classroom instruction with actual on-the-job experience at sponsoring auto and truck dealerships.

Though these certification programs are respected and highly valuable within the manufacturer's product line, they are seldom recognized with as much importance by a competitive manufacturer. For example, a Volkswagen technician would be required to retrain and recertify in a Toyota establishment.

**Colleges & Vo-Tech Schools**—There are a great many colleges and technical vocation schools that offer training in auto repair, paint and body shop repair and other related services. These courses, whether for certification or credit, are designed to teach basic principles and fundamentals, with the exception of the larger technical institutes and some of the full credit two- and four-year courses offered by colleges. The smaller community based programs attract the general public as well as beginning mechanics and serve the purpose of introducing the "fundamentals" to the novice, or those seeking a semi-apprentice position. Though they may claim that they are officially recognized with credentials, the fact is, most of them are not, and only count as partial or non-official programs. NIASE, for example, will award one year of work experience credit for three full years of high school auto shop training. They award one year work experience credit for two full years in a public or private trade school, technical institute, or four-year college program. For short course community programs, NIASE awards one month credit for every two months attended.

A few well known trade schools are NRI and Northwood Institute. Northwood is an accredited four-year college with campuses in Michigan, Texas, and Florida. Northwood, which is supported by the National Automobile Dealers Association (NADA), has a two-year Associate Degree program in automobile or truck marketing, automotive after-market management and automotive service management. It also offers a four-year Bachelor of Business Administration Degree.

# TYPES OF MECHANICS

Not all mechanics and technicians require the same training to satisfy the needs of the different repair facilities. There is a vast difference between the study and qualifications of a dealership technician and that of a "general service" mechanic who works in a chain or tire store. The size and popularity of a facility also has a direct bearing on what kind of budgets are allocated to train auto repair personnel. It is even possible that the attitude and image of the management staff have a direct bearing on what is required of their mechanics and technicians. The question of training ultimately affects the pay scale and motivation of individual mechanics. Hierarchy structures do exist throughout the facilities and this affects attitudes and the amount of professionalism each facility is capable of. It is important for you to know how these mechanics and technicians differ, and in what areas of repair and professional service they excel or do poorly. Consider the following categories a yard stick by which to measure the expertise of the different repair personnel.

**Department Store Mechanic**—For a long time, training films sufficed as the sole means of instruction for department store mechanics. Through repetition, mechanics acquired the skills that made them excellent "remove and replace" (R & R) mechanics. Heavy diagnostic thinking has never been part of the department store mechanic's program. So when it came to installing a battery, a set of tires, a brake job, an exhaust system, an alignment, or a tune-up, they were quite proficient. Nothing has changed much today. The department stores ordinarily train and certify their mechanics through their own educational programs, and provide their own local or regional instructors. Written tests have now become commonplace. But these brief tests and proficiency exams are not designed to cover the more indepth and major areas of auto repair, like engine overhaul and heavy transmission work. Rather, the mechanics are certified in specific areas such as brakes, front-end, tune-up and air conditioning.

Many of the mechanics are required to attend update training seminars, to watch films and discuss problem areas. Many department stores pay their mechanics to attend the additional training programs, even sending them out of state if necessary.

However, more often than not, it's literally a "nuts and bolts" issue with the department store mechanic. In essence, he is limited by what he has performed in the past. Mr. Hank Benck, Executive Director for the Automotive Service Association of Illinois, says that, "most of the department store chains are more interested in fast-selling components and services. In fact, the sales of parts play such a priority that it overshadows, in some cases, the profit margins brought about by labor. The 'in and out' concept holds true with the large department stores just as it does with the quick stops. Good engine rebuilding is time consuming. Also, the liability factors are too great to enter into more difficult repair areas. With the mechanics, emphasis is placed on replacing parts rather than on extending their training in technology."

The department store mechanic often works on a commission or bonus program, which is an incentive for him to sell additional parts over the prescribed work. His hourly wage varies but it falls somewhere between $4.50 per hour for a general service position, up to $8.00 or $9.00 per hour.

**Dealership Technician**—As mentioned before, dealership technicians are highly trained and professional. That is why they are referred to as a "technician" rather than as a "mechanic." Dealership technicians must attend extensive training seminars before they begin work, and thereafter, take frequent update seminars to keep current with new models and technical developments. Unlike private shops, these technicians are forced to take these seminars as a job prerequisite. They also have the finest equipment and tools at their disposal.

Another advantage you'll find with the dealership technician is that he doesn't work on any other type of car, and has seen many of the same problems time and time again.

Most dealership mechanics fancy themselves as the highest form of technician. They are everything but an R & R mechanic. They are diagnosticians. Technical troubleshooters. Scientists. Craftsmen. But never referred to in the trade as "mechanics." They are paid extraordinary sums for performing some of the same tasks that other mechanics undertake. Most are licensed and certified. Most dealership technicians are NIASE certified, experienced and know every nut and bolt on their make of car.

He is not forced to sell, because the selling of parts and additional service are left to the service manager or service writer, therefore you will rarely, if ever, deal with him directly.

A dealership technician is required to attend update training seminars on a constant and regular basis. This includes studying manufacturer's new parts, industry bulletins, and attending specially sponsored training programs. Some dealerships institute rigid "refresher" courses that are intended to aid the technicians in passing their reclassification courses to keep their licenses and certificates current.

**Chain Store Mechanic**—These mechanics are paid an hourly wage (not much more than department store types), and many of them operate off of the previously mentioned bonus and commission system that breeds dishonesty. The more parts they sell, and the higher number of cars they turn out, the more they make.

Most of the mechanics are certified through their own company program, and are sometimes sent to class sessions and instruction. A good percentage of chain store mechanics in California have smog licenses issued by the State Bureau of Automotive Repair. Sometimes a chain store will work with outside agencies such as The National Institute For Automotive Service Excellence, The Automotive Information Council, and The Automotive Service Association (all affiliated), to schedule periodic testing for the issuance of licenses and certification. An NIASE certified mechanic is not often found in a chain store because such certification would entitle him to higher pay than that offered by chain stores.

The sheer volume, quick turnaround time and bonus and commission pay scale forces the chain store mechanic to work at a hectic pace, which often leads to slipshod work and costly mistakes. Accidents happen. Any time there is high volume auto repair coupled with a commission or bonus system, the by-product will be greed and carelessness. The customer suffers because he is prey to mechanics who have to sell parts to achieve bonus pay.

The chain store mechanic performs mostly R & R work, and is not usually experienced in repairs involving internal work on major components such as transmissions, engines, clutches and chassis. Like the department store mechanic, this mechanic can be very good at what he does—R & R repair. He learns mostly through repetition, especially in the tire and muffler chains, because the process for removing and installing tires and mufflers is just about the same for any make of car. This doesn't give the chain store mechanic a lot of motivation to improve beyond this level, nor do most companies give them the incentive. Corporate training programs are not usually enforced in the chain stores past the point of initial certification or "checkout" in certain repair areas, because if the chain store mechanic were to progress beyond this point, he'd probably move on to a more demanding, higher paying job.

**Service Station Mechanic**—Whether or not a service station mechanic is licensed and certified is something you'd have to check for yourself. Smog licenses must be openly displayed by the management—this is state law. Too frequently it does not apply to other credentials. If he has gained proficiency and holds other credentials he will usually hang them up to show proof of expertise. A few of the larger service station chains have NIASE mechanics, but it is not likely. Heavy R & R work in a typical gas station is uncommon. This is due to their limited resources, heavy competition and poor employee prospects. The owner/manager might be the only person in the station who holds any type of certification or license, and even this is subject to question.

It is common for a service station mechanic to work on a 40/20 commission deal. This is a labor and parts package that allows the mechanic to keep 40% of the actual labor money that he performs plus 20% of the parts that he sells or causes the shop to sell. Many times he is given a choice. He can accept either a high hourly wage or he can work on the labor and parts program. Invariably, many of them choose the commission. At some service stations the owners give them no choice and offer the commission-only option. This labor and parts commission deal is just as deadly as the bonus system that department and chain stores employ. It works by the same principles. It's also to the station owner's advantage to let the mechanic sell as much as he can.

To be sure there are some service station mechanics who are old veterans and really care about the condition of your car as well as your wallet. Some of these mechanics have been working in the same spot for over twenty years. These mechanics know every one of their customers by name along with the peculiarities of their cars. Quite often, the owner is also the mechanic, service writer, cashier and gas pumper!

**Quick Stop Mechanics**—To call a quick stop employee a mechanic is a bit of a stretch. He is overworked and underpaid. He is undertrained. But he is in high demand because he will work so hard for so little. These mechanics are the lowest paid in the business.

Oil change, tune-up and smog check might be their strong suit but their expertise in other areas of repair should be questioned.

Surprisingly, quick stop mechanics could be very eager to pursue additional outside training courses in their sincere desire to move on. They soon discover that their wages are too low for the amount of work they are producing, and their chances for advancement are not likely to improve. Training provided by the management would be sparse, if any.

**Specialty Shop Mechanic**—Here you might find a "diamond in the rough," especially in foreign car repair. A specialty shop technician generally really cares about what he does, and has a deep appreciation for the cars he specializes in. He fancies himself as a craftsman and adopts an approach to his business as such.

Many of these mechanics have probably come from the dealerships and set up their own shops, possibly taking some of their fellow technicians along with them. Their familiarity with a specific make of car allows them to diagnose and solve problems quickly.

Most specialty shop technicians hold the licenses and certifications that a dealership technician would, such as NIASE certification. New employees in specialty shops are expected to participate in these training and testing programs in order to advance into journeyman positions or serve beginning apprenticeships and to maintain the high standards set by the owners. The technicians are paid a flat hourly rate for prescribed work. Nevertheless, the hourly rate is very high, better than all other facilities except the dealership.

You're likely to get some of the best, and most honest service from a specialty shop because they rely heavily on reputation and word of mouth. They don't have the huge marketing and advertising support of large dealerships and mega chain and department stores. The technicians might have more direct contact with the customer, even though service managers are responsible for this association.

Specialty shop technicians also are very good about keeping abreast of the technological advances in the cars they specialize in.

## SUPPORTING PLAYERS

Aside from the mechanic, there are other people you'll deal with. In fact, depending on the facility, you may never get to deal with the mechanic or meet him. In large repair organizations, your car can change hands as many as a half a dozen times, traveling an assembly line before it is done. You should know exactly who is handling each area, why, and what are their limitations, duties and areas of expertise. There are channels of authority that you must be aware of in solving the root of the complaint (if you have one), as well as asking service advice and other questions. Who holds the power in most shops? Who is really the boss? How high up must you go to resolve a serious customer satisfaction complaint?

Conversely, in smaller shops, i.e., gas stations and quick stops, there might be only one or two individuals that you deal with, and depending upon whom, you will have to know which one is responsible for your ultimate satisfaction.

**The Service Manager**—He or she can be called a shop foreman, service writer, service manager, general manager, department store manager, or "owner." He is directly responsible to the establishment for income, contact with the public and the general welfare of its employees. He is the boss from whom the mechanic must take direction. Most first impressions of a repair facility will be made by this one person.

Managers can be fine-tuned individuals, molded and bred from managerial schools, but more often they have worked their way up from "lot lizard." Though some mechanics make excellent managers, it is not true that most managers have been mechanics at one time. Not full-line mechanics, at any rate. While it is preferred to have a manager with mechanical aptitude and skills, as well as a general knowledge of auto parts, it is not a prerequisite. In many shops a mechanic is discouraged from seeking a managerial position. Though he has the technical knowledge of repair procedures, he often lacks the right personality for the job.

The manager is the one who gives the estimate and has you sign the repair order, and dealing with him is therefore seen as a necessary evil. Customers often believe the service manager, not the mechanic, is responsible for your repair bill, when in truth both are.

Managers are under a lot of pressure. Not only must they deal with distraught, suspicious and irritated customers, but they are also faced with controlling the bottom line, inventory, scheduling and shop personnel. He is often under pressure to maintain and increase preset repair quotas, and this pressure can lead him astray.

You will deal with service managers in large repair facilities such as dealerships, specialty shops, chain and department stores, and even in some muffler shops and quick stops. The service manager will be the person who writes up your initial repair invoice and assigns your car to a specific mechanic. The mechanic diagnoses or confirms the work to be done, and often recommends additional repairs (be they necessary or unnecessary). The service manager then tries to convince you to have the additional repairs made, and to sign for the estimate that just rocked you back on your heels. He depends on the accuracy of a diagnoses from the mechanic; he does not usually make repair diagnoses or tests himself, unless they are very simple.

**Service Advisors & Writers**—In large facilities and most dealerships, you'll be greeted and checked out by a service advisor or writer, who is not a manager nor a mechanic, but the person responsible for getting down all of your repair problems and writing them up on a repair order. He is a middleman, and generally operates on some commission, therefore it is to his advantage to sell you additional service that you may not need. He'll tell you that they'll check the brakes for free. When he does that, you may expect a call from him to get you to authorize additional repairs. If you have a problem, it starts with this person, but doesn't end with him. That's for the service manager.

**Lot Lizard**—This is the lowest form of life in a large chain, department store or dealership. It is a person, usually a young teenage boy, who is required to perform odd jobs such as "gassing up" and washing customer's cars. He is also the one who will most likely deliver your car to you. Many times they are directed by mechanics to perform menial tasks, such as cleaning up spills, sweeping, cleaning parts and tools. What you don't want to see is the lot lizard under the hood of your car with tools in his hand.

**Parts Manager**—The parts manager directs work and manages the parts department. Parts managers typically work at dealerships where a large stockroom of parts is needed for repair. He usually directs a number of parts men who take part orders from mechanics. You would deal with him if you wanted to purchase a dealer part to take to another, less expensive but trusted facility to install. You'd also deal with him if you had to return the same part because it was faulty or defective.

**Department Manager**—Department managers are usually found in department stores. His counterpart at a dealership would be a general manager. They have authority over the service manager in that they must run both the outside repair facility and the inside auto parts floor or department, or the entire dealership in that case. He will direct all employees in sales and repair. His main subordinates are the service manager and the sales floor manager, who he must coordinate to keep both departments functioning smoothly. A complaint that cannot be resolved with the service manager can many times be solved by the department manager.

# 3

# GETTING STARTED

## Be prepared and don't sign the order just yet

You have finally decided where to get the car fixed, and have an idea as to the type of person you're going to be dealing with. But before you go on over to the facility, you'll need to gather more information to get prepared. One of the first things you should do is collect as much service information about your car as possible, such as when it last had a tune-up, when the oil was changed last and warranty information (especially if you're going to a dealership). Above all, read your owner's manual and determine the recommended maintenance intervals for such things as inspections, oil changes, tire rotations, brake jobs, etc. Why? Because no matter what the problem is, you're going to be pressured into buying extra service. That's the first and foremost job of a service manager or service writer—to sell you as many parts and as much service as he or she can. If he absolutely recommends an oil change, and you know that it was just changed 1500 miles ago and know it isn't due for another 2,000 miles according to the manual, then you'll be able to tell him no, you don't want it done. So before you head out the door, read over all of this paperwork so you'll be prepared.

# STEREOTYPES

Many repair facilities, just like salesmen, classify their "targets" and group them into stereotypes. How you are treated depends on how you are viewed. There are definite exceptions within every category, but these are observations based on my own experience as a service manager and mechanic. Let's take a look at some of these stereotypes, and see if you fall into any one of them.

## FAMILY MAN

High on the list of preferred customers are family men. A family man is more likely to follow the "book," when it comes to periodic maintenance and repair. If his vehicle is new or near new, the family man is more inclined to follow the recommendations of the manufacturer, and more often than not take the car to the dealership every time.

The problem is, the service managers prey on this sense of regularity and loyalty. They will often use the line "well—it is recommended by the manufacturer," when selling the family man service he hadn't thought of. Also, because he is a family man, he is often told that "he should have the brakes done or the tires changed for the safety of his family." With thoughts of brake failure occurring while negotiating a mountain incline with a car load of his kids, the family man often will sign for the additional brake inspection or tire rotation without giving it much further thought.

## SENIOR CITIZENS

Oddly enough, senior citizens are taboo with the dishonest repair facility. Like the family man, they are also inclined to be prompt and reliable customers, and it is not uncommon for them to remain with a car repair facility for years, as long as they feel they are being treated fairly and with honesty. They generally never miss an oil change or tune-up interval. One miss in the engine and they head straight for the shop.

Service managers and mechanics generally avoid pulling anything on seniors because seniors are often well-versed with the service intervals and manufacturer's recommendations in the manual. They know the book, and are likely to question everything, especially prices because many live on a fixed income. When told their car needs additional service, a senior is much more likely to demand concrete proof before signing the repair bill than other stereotypes.

Seniors are also more likely to follow through with a formal complaint or lawsuit. There are exceptions, of course, but most managers and mechanics have learned that it is unwise to outfox the wise.

# TEENAGERS

The service manager, on the whole, does not have a lot of patience with teenagers. For one thing, the feeling has always prevailed that the teenage driver has just about enough coin to put in his gas tank, never mind for a serious or light car repair. And, if I were a teen, I would do everything to perpetuate this myth. I would not, under any condition, let the service manager or mechanic know that my parents were helping out with the repair bill. In fact, I would make sure that they knew I was paying for it regardless. If a manager or mechanic knows for a fact that the kid isn't paying for it, then they are much more likely to sign him up for the maximum service.

Teenage boys, in particular, are difficult to fool, because unlike most teenage girls, who at best might have a passing interest in the mechanics of their car, boys are generally passionate about every nut and bolt.

In fact, most teenagers, especially boys, take their cars to a repair facility as an absolute last resort. Even girls will probably have had a boyfriend try and fix it first. They'll fumble and falter, and if it still isn't right, finally take it to a shop. Then, the mechanic is often confronted with homemade repairs made with homemade tools that need to be fixed before the real problem can be solved. Many teens try to install their own stereos, and end up making an electrical mess of the wiring. Quite often they'll modify the engine with aftermarket performance items such as camshafts and superchargers or add tires and rims that are too wide. Then the teenager ends up paying much more than he or she would have if they had gone to a repair shop right away.

So teenage boys end up putting a service manager in a difficult dilemma. Here's a repair that requires additional time to fix, which means extra "flag time," and a bigger ticket. But who's going to pay for it? In my experience as a manager, the young service customer will openly argue over the smallest repair bill, believing that he has been taken, or rooked in the deal somehow. Sadly enough, there is a practice too often used by the manager to rid the shop of a disgruntled teen who lacks funds, or has brought a modified wreck to the shop. He simply tells the customer after the inspection that the car is beyond "specs," "too modified," or "flunks" in some area. "Nope. Our policy won't cover it. Sorry, we're not licensed for that. None of my mechanics will touch it. Why don't you try so and so down the road..." These are stock phrases commonly used to avoid performing any repairs the teenager may not be able to afford. My advice to teens is to consult with a repair facility before attempting any modifications or repairs. With modifications, you may run into legal problems when it comes time a smog check. Many types of modifications will cause a car to fail a smog test.

## WOMEN

Unlike the teen who might be deliberately flunked out of a shop, a woman will face an entirely different problem. Though I have always tried to dispel the rumor that women are "stung" more often than any other customer in the auto repair industry, it is my conclusion that they are still prey to the mechanic and manager, although the single, young professional male is gaining more prominence as a "pigeon."

It used to be that women were openly taken advantage of in the auto repair industry—terribly so. But it is becoming much more difficult to try and pull the wool over their eyes. New research has shown that single women are much more discriminating and more informed when it comes to auto purchase and repair than are most men. But most women don't want anything to do with it physically. The degree of their distaste for the occupation can be keenly gauged by an observant service manager. A woman's dress and her attitude, can be a determining factor on how much she will ultimately pay for her repair. I'm not talking about a reputable and honest repair shop; I'm talking about the repair shops that would "scalp" women. A woman who walks daintily into a repair shop, wearing a business suit or dress, with high heels, a Louis Vuitton purse, custom nails and hair, who quickly signs an inspection invoice, saying "Gee, something's funny when I step on the brake," then rushes off to go shopping, is asking for a financial pummeling. A woman who projects this image, plus hands over her car keys, signs an estimate, and runs off because she does not like the atmosphere of the shop nor its inhabitants, runs the risk of being treated like a *lady*. And if this lady has flashed plastic (credit cards) at the service desk, she's likely to get more than a lady-like bill.

By dressing down and appearing more casual you can avoid the impression that you should pay more. A woman should not give the impression that her car repair is a major inconvenience that she doesn't want to deal with, nor that she is overly concerned with its probable expense.

In the worst cases, I've seen mechanics who blatantly rip off women more than any other type of customer, believing still that they know nothing about their car, and don't want to know. By projecting an image that you are concerned, informed and on your guard, you'll be much better off.

## SINGLE MALE PROFESSIONALS

Single, young, male professionals, sometimes referred to with the "Y" word, are another favorite target. Only with some obvious variations. Bachelors, particularly if they are executive and successful types, need to play down their airs of high status and importance when approaching a repair facility. Successful bachelors often have a life-style that consumes many priorities at once. Their indifference or preoccupation with business can stand in their way of monitoring their car repair. The businessman who is always in a hurry sets himself up for a high repair invoice because he's telling the manager that he doesn't have the time to deal with this problem and he just wants it taken care of no matter what it costs. If you've got the money to burn, fine, but you probably wouldn't be reading this book if that were the case.

As with women, it's not a bad idea for him to familiarize himself with the working parts of his car, to thoroughly read the owner's manual and even a few repair manuals. A little knowledge and understanding goes a long way when confronted by a mechanic who is trying to sell you extra service by using confusing auto jargon.

Dressing down when visiting an auto repair shop applies to the bachelor as well. A three-piece suit is a little on the over-kill side for a Saturday visit to the repair shop.

## GETTING AN ESTIMATE

Okay, you're waiting in line to see the service manager, and when called, you step up to the counter. Your first task is to describe to him the nature of your car's problem as accurately as possible. A good service manager will prompt you with questions to try and pinpoint what is wrong. He should be listening carefully and taking notes. He should not be taking personal phone calls or interrupting you and stepping into the back room every few minutes. In fact, he should be adopting the professional attitude of a doctor who is trying to determine your illness (And why not? He charges almost as much, right?).

---

**HINT**

*Several chapters of the American Automobile Association (AAA) offer their members a diagnostic service. The member brings his car down to the center and an AAA certified mechanic will inspect and diagnose the car. The AAA mechanic will give the member a printout listing the problem, and the recommended parts and services needed to correct it, but will not perform the actual repairs. The member can then take the printout to a repair facility and request that the recommendations be followed on the printout. This policy certainly helps to reduce the chances of unfair practices. If you are a member of the AAA, check with your local chapter to see if they provide this valuable service.*

---

If you're not treated with courtesy and respect, if the manager is disinterested or too casual about your problem, then you should take this as a sign that you may not have chosen well.

So now the manager scribbles some more, hands you a slip of paper, tells you the charges and when you can pick it up. So you sign on the dotted line, right? WRONG! You are entitled to an estimate and visual inspection first. The manager should ask to see your car. He should listen to it, or examine the general area, even test drive it before he starts writing up charges on the repair order (the exceptions would be a simple lube, oil and filter change, smog check or other regular maintenance procedure). If he doesn't offer it, demand it. If he still doesn't move from behind the counter or have a mechanic do it, then thank him very much for his time and go somewhere else.

**Inspection**—If the mechanic or service manager agrees to inspect the car, *go with him* if at all possible. Don't wait in the lounge for him to come back. Watch him as he inspects every inch of your car. If the inspection is in the service bay, stand outside the yellow line and watch the inspection take place. Part of a mechanic's or service manager's job in this inspection is to spot other areas they can sell you service on, or to "find" something wrong. Don't take the service manager's word for it when he says he looked at your tires when he was looking at the muffler and decided you need a tire rotation and balance for an extra $40.00. Ask him to show you the evidence (for more on tires, turn to chapter 4).

Furthermore, this inspection should be free of charge. Remember, this is not a diagnosis, for which you may be charged, but an estimate of what it will cost to find and fix the problem. Don't panic if the manager or mechanic writes up an invoice anyway. It is standard procedure for many places to account for every vehicle that comes into the shop. If they find the problem and you agree to come back later (always say you will come back later even if you don't intend to), he will release you with an "N/C" on your invoice. This means no charge and it is very common. If under the same circumstances a different shop charges you $25.00 for a few minutes inspection/diagnosis time, I would refuse to pay it unless they had specified the charges up front before they looked at your car. I would also never return to that shop again!

**Pressure**—Each area of R & R (Remove & Replace) repair has its own set of common shams and scams. For specifics, turn to the appropriate chapters. But there are some general tactics often employed to get you to sign for a high repair bill at this stage.

For instance, if the manager has quoted you a price, and your car is sitting up on the lift in the service bay with the wheels off, the manager is apt to say, "If you'll just sign here, we'll get started, heck the car's already half apart, we might as well get going." Or, the manager might say, "I'd take care of it right away if I were you. If you drive it any more, the problem's going to get worse and then it'll be even more expensive to fix." This may be true if you've got a severe oil leak or pre-ignition (detonation) problems, or possibly a broken wheel bearing or snapped tie-rod where the wheel's likely to fall off, but not so with most R & R problems. Don't fall for this tactic. If the car made it to this facility, it will get you to the one down the street. Don't be intimidated by the heavy sighs and groans the service manager (often referred to as SM) will emit, making you feel as though you've really ruined his day by making him put those wheels back on (which you didn't ask to have taken off, by the way) because you won't sign the repair order. There is nothing written that says you have to commit to repairs because the shop performed a free inspection.

## THE REPAIR ORDER

Commonly called the "R.O." the repair order is a *legal document*, a contract that says you are authorizing the facility to perform the repairs listed and that you agree to, and will be held liable for, the charges and rates listed. It also says the repair facility will perform those repairs as stated. If you have any doubts about the work to be done and how you're going to be charged for it, now is the time to ask questions, before you sign.

The repair order should list the following: a very accurate description of the problem; the list of replacement parts to be used and their *actual* charges; the amount of labor time estimated to complete the job and the rate charged per hour for the labor; any and all machine work to be performed; your name, address and phone numbers where you can be reached.

**Parts**—You should question the service manager as to whether the parts used are in stock or must be sent out for, and whether or not they are generic replacements or factory original parts. Ask what the price differences are between the two. You want to make sure you're not being charged for factory parts when generics are going to be used. Second, make sure the repair order states that the parts to be used are covered under some sort of warranty. Most reputable repair shops will offer some sort of warranty, the usual being 90 days.

**Labor**—Quite often, the amount per hour for labor varies with the type of work. For instance, the charge for body repair work may be higher than that for a tune-up. The facility should have a "rate" card listing the different charges for different types of work. If this is how they operate, then make sure you compare the work to the rate listed to make sure you're not being overcharged. Furthermore, every repair facility is supposed to estimate the amount of time a certain job should take, based on a "flat rate manual." A *Mitchell Flat Rate Repair* manual is the most common one used. If something seems to require an inordinate amount of time, question the service manager about it and ask to see his flat rate manual where it says so. If he gives you the runaround, thank him for his time, take the estimate and tell him you wish to think about it, and motor on down the road.

---

## CAUTION

*The shop flat rate manual, which contains maximum allowable shop labor costs for individual repair services can be, and still is, a devastating device used by most repair facilities to obtain the highest labor costs from the consumer. For example, a dealership flat rate manual can stipulate that a brake job will be 2.5 hours of time, and at their labor charge of $42.00 an hour the total labor (less parts) will be $105.00. What they don't tell you is that the mechanic almost always finishes such a repair in 3/4 or 1/2 the allowed time, but you are still charged the full flat rate cost prescribed by the book. Hence, with the development of new tools and techniques, the mechanic is finishing much faster, but you are still obligated to pay their "full time" labor cost. The "hood-up" syndrome is a direct by-product of this practice (finishing the work too early).*

---

**Other Services**—Repair or maintenance work other than what you specified has a nasty habit of creeping into a repair order that is too quickly signed by a rushed customer. Look at the list of work to be done very carefully. Question any procedure that is written in confusing "autospeak." Refer to the glossary at the back of this book to check out some of the words. The manager should clearly explain each one. If you didn't come in for an oil change, then make sure you don't see "L.O.F." on the repair order. Once you sign for the work and it is done, it's difficult to get out of having to pay for it.

**Machine Work**—You should only be charged for additional machine work if it is farmed out to another facility. If the shop has the equipment in-house, like a brake lathe machine for turning drums and rotors, but you're being charged an extra price for it, question the manager about it. If the facility advertised a $49.95 brake job that included turning drums and rotors, how come you're suddenly being charged an additional $25.00 for machine work?

**Troubleshooting**—Aside from the dealerships, most repair facilities do not charge for diagnosis or "troubleshooting," especially for simple "R & R" work. Let's face it, if you drive in to the repair shop and your car sounds like a tank, it doesn't take a rocket scientist to figure out that you need a new muffler. Don't allow yourself to be charged for

---

troubleshooting simple remove and replace items.

On the other hand, troubleshooting charges may be warranted for a mystical electrical problem that will require several hours of checking wire leads, grounds, fuse boxes, transistors, etc. to locate.

**Authorization**—The repair order should state (generally in fine print) that the facility will perform *only* the work specified on the repair order unless authorized by you to perform any other additional repairs. In other words, they can't just decide to fix something else if they should find it without first contacting you to get your okay. If that's not stipulated loud and clear, then write it on yourself before you sign.

---

## CAUTION

*If you receive a call from the repair facility stating they found something else and recommend repairing it, I would proceed with caution. If possible, tell them that you'll be over to discuss the problem with them. If it's a damaged part that needs to be replaced, tell them you want to see it first. Ask how much the additional charge will be. Ask how necessary the repair is at this time. If you can't go over, and the repair is not absolutely necessary, then I would tell them you don't want to have it done right at that moment and ask them to proceed with the authorized repair only. Then jot down this conversation on a note pad in case you need it later.*

---

**Price Haggling**—Quite often the price offered for the repair is not what the facility will take. Most facilities do have some margin to work with. I know of a friend who went to a chain muffler facility to have the muffler replaced. After putting the car on the rack, the mechanic performed a quick inspection, then took my friend to look under the car and showed him the repairs needed. The car was imported, so the mechanic explained they would have to make a custom exhaust system consisting of three pieces and some additional hangers. The original muffler was a one piece unit connected to the tailpipe, and was only available as such from the dealer. The price was just under $200! My friend was stunned and told the mechanic that he simply couldn't afford such a price. My friend also suggested he would have to take the car somewhere else. The mechanic told him to wait a moment in the front lounge while he worked with the figures to see what he could do. Ten minutes later, the mechanic reappeared and had adjusted the estimate, lowering the amount by over $50! However, my friend still didn't sign because he knew he was being taken. In this case, all the facility had to do was cut off the old muffler and attach a new one with an adapter. This is a common scam pulled on import car owners that is covered in greater detail in chapter 5.

Don't fall for one of the service manager's favorite scams. Quite often, they may tell you that the estimate listed is high just in case something should happen, but he doubts very much that it won't go that high at all. Rest assured that you'll be told that "something did happen" when you come to get your car and the final amount is the same as the estimate.

**Deposits**—Some facilities demand a deposit, usually 10% of the estimate, when you sign the R.O. I think this is ridiculous. They have the keys to your car! How much more of a deposit could they possibly want! I would politely inform them of this, and if that wasn't enough, take your car somewhere else.

**Final Note**—If you decide to go ahead and sign, make sure you keep a copy of the repair order with you at all times until the repair is finished. This is in case the shop should call to ask you about additional repairs, or to discuss the work they are doing. You'll need the repair order as a reference. After the repair is done, file the repair order away along with all other service receipts for as long as you keep your car.

## A SECOND OPINION

If the amount of the repair order still seems to shatter all common sense despite a thorough explanation from the service manager, and you've tried to haggle with the price without success, you still have an option—you can get a second opinion. Second opinions work extraordinarily well in auto repair because mechanics have an ironic habit of burning down another mechanic's diagnosis, or dismissing it altogether. Mechanics often exhibit a "battle of wills," and frequently compete against each other. A mechanic that performs a second or third opinion for you (once you've told him about your first diagnosis), is more inclined to find out what you really need, or how he can go about beating the repair cost of the previous diagnosis. He knows that if he can be honest with you and save you legitimate dollars, you might come back to him in the future. So his theory is, find that basic problem, do just enough to fix it, save the customer substantial dollars, and voila! That customer will be his, probably for good. How they treat you the next time might be a different story altogether. The important point is to let them show off, get that reduced deal, then vacate the premises with money in your pocket.

Let's set up a typical scenario. Mechanic A has test-driven your vehicle, inspected it on the rack, and he has deduced that the slop in the steering wheel and the poor turning response, are due to a defective steering box gear. The gears are worn, and this is what's giving you that extra play or "lash." He says that the parts and labor will run about $350, and the wait for the part, since it is a dealer item, might be a few days. He'll ask that you sign the repair estimate so they can get started because you don't want to wait with such a dangerous problem. That should be your cue to politely ask for a copy of the written estimate so you can think about it some more, and that you need to make arrangements to leave the car, get the money, etc. Then head for another repair shop. You tell mechanic B what mechanic A told you about your vehicle. You will innocently proclaim that "it's always a wise move to get a second opinion," and that "I didn't quite trust the other mechanic's diagnosis." You would like mechanic B to double-check the gear box and tell you what he thinks.

Mechanic B says, "Oh, those idiots down at that (expletive deleted) rip-off garage have made mistakes before."

He then goes on to do the second inspection. He needs to impress you with his skill and reasoning so he will try very hard to refute the first claim. If he does find the gear box bad he will tell you so but probably beat the first price. Or, if you were being scammed, he might find the real problem.

Now, mechanic B says, "Just as I thought. It's not the gear box, but an *adjustment* to the gear box. I loosen this cap-nut, turn this screw and voila! It takes out the excess lash in the steering box. You see, that's what the adjusting screw is there for. There's no need to buy a *whole* gear box. Just a case of average wear."

In this case, mechanic B just might send you off down the road after making a one-minute adjustment without charging you anything. He wants you to remember him—forever.

What have we learned here? Well, just maybe mechanic A knew what the real problem was only his receipts were low for that week, or his bonus figures didn't look too good. So he was going fishing hoping

---

## HINT

*A few shops have instigated a "clock in/clock out" method of determining shop labor costs. That means that a mechanic must punch a time card at the beginning of a labor service and at the end of it. The elapsed time on the card is truly what you pay in labor charges according to their hourly labor charge. Using the example of the brake job on page 46, if the mechanic finished the repairs in 1 1/2 hours, the labor charge would be $63.00, or the "true" time that the mechanic spent on the repairs. You can see the dramatic difference in these two policies. There are not many shops that have the "clock in/clock out" policy, but you would be wise to call up beforehand to see if they did.*

that you would spring for the complete repair job. You didn't believe his extravagant estimate, and instead paid a visit to mechanic B. Mechanic B will snag you as a customer and play it straight this time. That will show mechanic A a thing or two! Naturally, you don't care about how the mechanics or shops feel about each other, only in getting the best possible, most honest repair job for your car. But in this instance, do you see how one played against the other and you came out on top? Try this method and see how well it works. Even third and fourth opinions are justified when you are confronted with a very high repair estimate.

## SCARE TACTICS

With no great pride I am going to divulge to you what has been a blot on the automotive industry since time immemorial. They have commonly been called "scare or boo tactics," although there is nothing ghostly about the term. Basically, a "boo" tactic is a deceptive diagnosis used to frighten the customer into purchasing a part or service that he believes will either save his life, or prevent major expense in the future. Such a claim is hardly justified, especially when the manager warns you that if you do not purchase a certain part you are likely to end up in some horrendous accident as a result of your negligence.

Some of these claims are legitimate. But most of them are not. Most often they are employed when a mechanic has performed an inspection on your vehicle (in addition to prescribed work) and found something that is, or can be, a potential problem. What's worse, if you are not standing around monitoring the work on your car, you are bound to get a "flash" (additional) inspection whether you like it or not. Even if you came in for an air cleaner, there is a good chance that your car will be racked, the wheels removed (to check brakes), the suspension scrutinized and your tires gauged. The cost of the air cleaner is chump change compared with what the manager would like to get out of you as a result of this flash inspection. A dishonest shop will employ a seek and destroy mission to find something wrong with a vehicle, and then blow the diagnosis way out of proportion and reason. The customer is relieved when he hears that there is nothing that he has done to make his car a hazard to humanity, but when told that the fatigue on his parts will sooner or later lead to mechanical failure or worse, most customers are scared right into signing an invoice for the additional work. The customer is apt to believe the diagnosis without question. The manager is counting on customer ignorance to get as much parts and service as he can.

**Correct Warnings**—Some of these warnings may be justified, however. For instance, if the steel belt of a radial tire is showing through the tire tread, (the sidewall area being most common), you do increase the chances of a rapid blow-out, which can lead to a life-threatening accident. A severe leak of brake fluid in your master cylinder or wheel cylinder can cause a sudden loss of brake pedal pressure, thus leading to a collision. If per chance one of your front end parts is so worn that it approaches the point of breakage, this can cause an immediate loss of steering and lead to a collision. If your carb linkage is hanging up, this can lead to an unexpected full throttle condition that could send you speeding into another vehicle.

All these examples are legitimate and life-threatening concerns, but usually there is a warning of some type before they deteriorate or fail totally. Bad tires are visually discovered. Bad brakes are commonly found in the action of the brake pedal, or by a grating noise. Bad front end parts are usually felt in the steering response. Faulty carburetor linkage can usually forewarn a driver by abnormal acceleration or rpm's (revolutions per minute, very high idle).

But don't take the mechanic's or service manager's word for it! You have every right to demand a demonstration or to be shown the faulty part. If specifications are given, ask where those specs come from, ask to see them. If the mechanic or service manager hesitates, then it's likely they're leading you on.

Ironically, most managers don't have the ability to pursue the reason for the diagnosis past a rehearsed line. If you question them further and in detail about a specific cause-and-effect there is a good chance they will either skirt the issue, hesitate or excuse themselves to go ask a mechanic. If you are doubtful about how essential a replacement part or service is for your car, seek another opinion. Don't feel that you are obligated to agree with the shop staff simply because they make a recommendation to you. Use sound judgment and common sense. If you truly believe that a part cannot wait, and as a result you will be in jeopardy without it, go ahead and okay the repair.

✔ Be careful how you dress when you go into a repair facility. Be casual, play down your status. Don't appear rushed, in a hurry, greatly inconvenienced or disinterested in your repair. You should project just the opposite.

✔ Demand a free inspection and estimate once you've described the problem as accurately as possible. Go with the service manager if possible while he inspects the car.

✔ If the manager appears disinterested, leave.

✔ Don't be pressured into on-the-spot repairs just because they inspected your car for you at no charge.

✔ Don't sign the repair order until you've given it a thorough examination. Make sure it lists all parts, the hourly rate, the estimated number of hours. Keep a sharp eye out for "other" services listing unnecessary repairs.

✔ Write on the repair order that you won't authorize any increase over the estimate without notification first.

✔ The price written down on the repair order is quite often not what they'll take.

✔ Don't fall for the scam line, "We always estimate high just in case, but I'm sure the repair won't go that high." Be assured that when you come to get the car, it did indeed go that high.

✔ If something like a simple tune-up is listed as an 8-hour job, a warning flag should go up. Ask to see the service manager's flat-rate manual.

✔ If you have the time, seek a second opinion. Play the mechanics' egos and desperation for your business off of each other.

✔ Watch out for "scare" tactics employed by managers. They often are lines that prey on your sense of safety.

# 4

# THE SMALL STUFF

## L.O.F., TIRES, BALANCE & ALIGNMENT

In this chapter I will examine some of the easily performed, or ordinary repair services, that are fairly risk free. They too have their glitches but the problems are less involved and point to fewer trouble spots. They will be mentioned because they are frequent services that are performed with average care. Occasionally, short cuts are taken because they are so easily performed. As viewed by many technicians and mechanics, they are mundane chores. They are performed every day by all mechanics and technicians to some degree. The risks aren't too serious with these services but if too many things are left out of a procedure they can result in annoying conditions and poor automobile performance.

## THE L.O.F. (LUBE, OIL, FILTER)

The lube, oil and filter should be the most frequent preventative maintenance chore you perform on your car. Engine oil is directly responsible for the lubrication of hundreds of moving parts in an engine. Without frequent and regular changes oil breaks down and becomes thin (loses its viscosity). It is subjected to tremendous heat and pressure. If allowed to become too dirty it can clog an oil filter and affect oil pressure directly. If oil changes are not performed with regularity and with high grade oils, engine wear can be expected to increase in direct proportion to the neglect.

## WHEN TO CHANGE THE OIL

When does the oil need to be changed? You can follow the recommended mileage intervals listed in your car owner's manual. Most all manuals suggest an oil change at regular intervals. But be aware those intervals are a general guideline based on average use. You may not be an average driver. If you commute long distance daily in hot weather, or tow frequent loads, or consistently drive well above the speed limit, then your oil may break down faster than average. Generally, when engine oil turns to a completely black color as shown on the dipstick, it's time to change it. Fresh oil is usually a dark amber, dark green or dark yellow color. When it's black, it's dirty and the viscosity has broken down. Also, as your car gets older, with more miles on the engine, the more frequently the oil should be changed. Cars with mileage over 100,000 miles should have the oil changed every 2,000 to 3,000 miles.

## TYPES OF OIL

Engine oil is engine oil, right? Not really. There are differences between the grades, and when you have the oil changed, you can usually pick the grade oil you want. If you don't specify, you'll get an "average" weight oil, which may not be what you want in some cases.

---

### CAUTION

*Insist on high quality, brand name oil and fluids. Quaker State, Pennzoil, Valvoline, and Havoline are examples of high quality oils. It might cost a few cents more, but the long-term benefits for engine life are increased. The generic ATF (automatic transmission fluid) that most quick stops provide is usually very good quality. Your owner's manual will have the exact information you need when considering any fluid change; the type, viscosity, brand name, etc.*

---

Some manufacturers require that you use SE-quality engine oil when making a change. Some oils are detergent and non-detergent, with the detergent oil being the most popular. You must consult your owner's manual to find out which is listed.

Different weights or *viscosities* of oil are used, such as: 5W-20, 5W-30,

10W, 10W-30, 10W-40, 20W-20, 20W-40, 20W-50, 40W and 50W. These relative thicknesses of oil can have an effect on your fuel economy. Lower thickness engine oils can provide increased fuel economy. Higher thickness engine oils are preferred for higher temperature weather conditions. Thicker oil breaks down slower in a hot engine whereas the lighter engine oils might give better gas mileage under moderate conditions. However, lighter weight oils break down faster in a hot environment, which could increase engine wear. You can refer to an oil viscosity chart, which may be available in some parts stores. It will list the oil weights that will provide the best balance of fuel economy, engine life and oil economy, under different temperature and driving conditions.

## OIL FILTERS

Oil filters are canisters containing fabric filtering elements. Located inline with the circulating oil, their purpose is to screen out debris and engine particles. Some of the popular filters are Fram (imports), AC-Delco (GM), Pennzoil, STP and Motorcraft (Ford). Most filters screw into a mounting plate located on the engine. They require an O-shaped rubber ring to seal them against their mount. The ring should be coated with a light film of oil before application, and the rule of thumb to tightening an oil filter is to tighten by hand until it stops, then go 1/4 turn farther.

## LUBRICATION

Lube refers to lubrication. The car's chassis and front-end parts are typically lubricated with grease, usually around the time that an oil change is performed. Some of the lubrication spots would be: the upper ball joints, lower ball joints, tie-rod ends, idler arm, Pitman arm and sometimes the U-joint on cars that have the fittings.

These fittings, or *zerks*, resemble small nipples and this is where the lube grease is injected, by means of a pressurized gun, or by a hand pump. The tie-rod ends and ball joints have boots or cups that cover the ball-and-socket joints. These cups hold extra grease in this area to provide lasting lubrication. If one of these rubber boots tears or breaks, grime, dirt and sand can contaminate the joint. This causes friction which leads to increased wear or allows water to saturate the joint and cause it to rust. Broken or torn boots should always be replaced. On newer cars you might see front end parts that do not have zerk fittings. These parts are "factory sealed" and do not require lubrication. If the part fails due to wear it is usually replaced as a unit.

# BEWARE OF THE GOOD DEAL

A typical advertisement for an L.O.F. special might look like this:

1. Drain oil and fill with up to 5 qts.
2. Replace filter.
3. Lubricate entire chassis.
4. Check all other fluid levels.

So you ask yourself what could go wrong with item number 1? Not much but I hope the mechanic knows precisely how much oil each and every make automobile holds: either four, five or six quarts. If oil is overfilled it increases oil pressure, putting strain on gaskets and front and rear main seals. It could then blow out one of these gaskets or seals and you'd have a serious oil leak and a costly repair involving the replacement of them. It's a good idea for you to know exactly how much oil your car requires, information that can be found in your owner's manual.

Next, I would certainly hope that the mechanic uses a box-end wrench or a socket to remove the oil drain plug. Using a crescent wrench strips the bolt plug. I would hope that he also replaces the plug washer, or retainer, if the old one is worn or scored.

**Wrong Filter**—What could happen in number 2? Well, if the wrong size filter is installed there will be a nice puddle on the floor when the engine is started, and the oil will soon blow all over the underside of the

## CAUTION

*Four items are removed and replaced or retightened during an oil/filter change. They are; the filler cap, the dipstick, the filter and the oil pan bolt. I would advise that you check these areas to make sure they were replaced and tightened properly. I would also recheck to make sure that the oil level is at the proper level, and that the oil appears to be clean and of a yellowish-green color, not black. Second, before you turn in the car for this service, note the type of filter on the car, and check to make sure that a different or new replacement of the original filter has been installed on the car afterward. During the hectic, repetitive pace of a quick stop facility, it is possible that the mechanics could overlook these areas, either intentionally or unintentionally. I've heard of many cases where the oil filler cap had been left off, or the oil wasn't filled properly, or that the filter was never replaced. A quick check will save you the hassle of an oily, smoking mess, and quite possibly major engine failure within minutes of picking up your car.*

car. If this goes undetected, you could be in for a rapid loss of oil pressure and a major engine rebuild. If oil has splashed on the exhaust pipe you might see and smell smoke when you drive your car away.

**The O-Ring**—New oil filters always come with a rubber gasket ring. When your old filter is removed sometimes the old gasket sticks to the surface of the mount; it does not come off with your filter. A mechanic might say "what the heck" and screw the new filter up against the old gasket ring and toss the new ring on the floor. It does happen. You paid for that part, didn't you? Why shouldn't it be installed? Furthermore, if the mechanic doesn't take it off and puts the new one on over the old one, the filter won't seal properly and you'll have a leak. Oil filters should be hand tightened, firmly, unless the oil filter is difficult to reach which would justify the use of an oil filter wrench. If your oil filter is overtightened, it could crush the housing of the oil filter, or possibly crush the gasket ring. If it was an old ring, it could leak.

**No Grease**—What about item number 3? The only problem that I have seen in this area is the mechanic's failure to reach a fitting, usually an upper ball joint, or he lets the pressure gun deliver too much grease which sometimes causes the boot or cup to explode. In either case, he should use care to remedy the problem.

**Checking Other Fluids**—Item number 4 is where most people are taken. This complimentary check is either overlooked or defined strictly. In other words, to check the fluids means to glance at them to see what level they are at. It doesn't mean adding them for free. The areas included are: the rear end or differential, automatic transmission fluid, manual transmission oil, power steering fluid, brake and clutch fluid, radiator or radiator reservoir (water), wiper/washer fluid and battery water. They'll tell you it is low, but if you want it filled, you'll be charged accordingly for each type of fluid. I know of some people who have been to a major quick stop chain where the advertised $19.95 special totaled out to be nearly $35.00. The sham here is that they weren't told this up front. They just went and filled the reservoirs without asking and charged them accordingly. To be sure, not all quick stops are like this, but it would behoove you to ask up front just what the special includes and what it doesn't.

That's not to say the fluids in these areas are not important. They are. But many of these areas (except for the manual transmission and differential) are easy to reach and you should be able to purchase some brake fluid, or coolant, from your local grocery or drug store at substantial savings and fill the area yourself. Then you'd have plenty of fluid left over for future refills. In fact, changing the oil and filter is a regular maintenance procedure you could easily perform yourself. For tips on how to do this, go to page 168.

# TIRES

The condition of your tires is directly related to safety. New tires are expensive regardless of the bargain price, therefore most people put off buying them until the last minute. Tires can affect steering response, cornering ability, noise, ride quality, road hazard resistance, rolling resistance, traction and fuel economy.

## SELF-DIAGNOSIS

Any automobile owner can visually inspect his tires for condition and road worthiness. You should replace your tires when they are worn if 2/32-inch, or less tread remains, or the cord is damaged, or if the belt material is showing through the sidewall.

**Tread Indicators**—Most tires have built-in tread indicators (wear bars) that appear between the tread grooves. Tires that are worn and expose these indicators should be replaced when the bar reaches across three or more grooves. The bars will look like a solid line running across the width of your tire. This means that there is not much tread left and the likelihood of poor handling or a hazardous blowout is increased. If the tire tread sidewall is weathered or cracked, cut or snagged deep enough to expose the cord or interior fabric, this would justify replacing that tire. That goes for bumps, bulges, splits, punctures, cuts, or any other injury it has sustained that appears abnormal.

You might notice a vibration in the steering wheel, one that seems to come and go depending on how fast you're going. This vibration could mean the tire is no longer balanced because the weight fell off. It could be a front end problem too.

Sometimes a tire will wear unevenly if it wasn't properly balanced or if the alignment is off. Look at your tires to see if the tread is more worn on one side than the other.

---

## CAUTION

*Always try to buy major brand name tires. Goodyear, Firestone, Michelin, General, Uniroyal, and BF Goodrich are examples of good quality tires. Under no circumstances should you purchase lesser quality tires or recaps at high prices, unless you specify this option. If you suffer road hazard damage to one of your tires, you can return to any store of the same chain (with invoice and certificate in hand) and have the repair or service adjusted at that store. It is not essential that you return to the same store from which you bought the tire. All stores must honor the standard agreement, and any store that does not is breaching your contract.*

---

# TIRE INFLATION

The cold inflation pressures listed on the tire placard provide the best balance of tire life, ride quality and vehicle handling (all under normal conditions).

The higher pressures indicated will result in improved fuel economy. Incorrect tire inflation can have adverse affects on tire life and vehicle performance. Low pressures result in increased tire flexing and overheating. This weakens the tire fabric and increases the chance of damage or failure. It can result in tire overloading, abnormal wear, erratic handling and reduced fuel economy. Too high an air pressure can result in abnormal wear, uncomfortable ride and increase the chance of damage from road hazards.

If a tire is worn on both the inside and outside it is probably due to underinflation. That is how underinflation wears tires on the inside and outside of a tire at the same time.

What about overinflation you say? Overinflation will wear just the middle of your tire, because when it has too much air, it bulges at that point—in the middle. The outsides of your tire might look great but say two tire treads or grooves are worn smooth in the middle of the tire. This would be overinflation and you couldn't confuse it with underinflation.

**Checking**—All car owners can check tire pressure with a tire pressure gauge. Radial tires, in particular, must be checked to avoid the assumption that they "look right." Even radial tires that are underinflated often "look right," but they might be lower in pressure by as much as 10 psi, and you would not know it unless a proper gauge was used. After checking the tires for pressure, reinstall the valve caps. These prevent dirt and moisture from getting into the valve core which could cause a leak.

Tire inflation pressures should be checked at least every 45 days, or when you plan to change the load factor, or take an extended trip. Always check tire pressures when the tires are "cold" (before driving). The "cold" tire inflation pressure applies to the tire that has not been used, or not driven for more than a few miles. Remember that it is normal for tire pressure to increase 4 to 8 pounds per square inch or more when the tires become hot from driving. This temperature expansion is normal. Do not reduce or bleed off tire inflation pressures after driving your car because this will underinflate your original "cold" setting. Exact tire pressure is critical and can wear tires faster than an alignment problem.

# TIRE ROTATION

Front and rear tires perform different jobs and can wear differently depending upon conditions and driving habits and whether the vehicle is front or rear wheel drive. That is why they should be rotated—moved to different locations of the vehicle to even out the load and wear responsibilities. Awhile back it was assumed that radial belted tires could be crossed or moved to the other side of the vehicle (some of the older owner's manuals display this procedure). But new research now shows that doing this can flex or twist a tire and cause a "radial pull." It is now recommended to rotate radial-belted tires from front to back or back to front.

---

## HINT

*Generally, tires should be rotated every 6,000 to 10,000 miles. Check your tire warranty invoice to see if a free rotation is included in the tire purchase. If you abide by its guidelines, your warranty should be strictly upheld. But this free rotation is often conveniently forgotten by the management of many tire stores unless you mention it to them.*

---

## REPLACEMENT

If your tires need to be replaced you should replace them with a similar size, design and make. On vehicles originally equipped with radial tires you will find a Tire Performance Criteria (TPC) specification number molded into the tire sidewall. This indicates that the tire meets certain size, performance and load standards which were developed specifically for your vehicle. It is important that you replace your tires with tires that conform to these standards as closely as possible. Putting on tires that don't meet these specifications could be dangerous.

**Mixing**—Don't mix tire makes when making a replacement. Tires come in bias, bias-belted and radial designs. Always stay with the same design—keep them in matched sets. If your tires are calibrated with the Alpha system you can usually change over to metric with a tire that is near or close enough to duplicate the original. A different size or type tire may affect ride, handling, suspension geometry, vehicle ground clearance, tire or tire chain clearance to the fender well and even speedometer/odometer readings.

In regard to speedometer readings, when you have put inappropriate tires on your car, you could be driving faster than your gauge indicates and vice versa. With smaller replacement tires than original, you could notice decreased fuel economy and blame the reason on some other component on your vehicle. In replacing a single tire it should be paired on the same axle with the least worn tire of the other three, preferably on the front of the vehicle.

**Balancing**—When purchasing a new set of tires it is best to have them balanced at the same time they are mounted to your wheels. This will guard against uneven wear from the onset. Tires that are not balanced can create many different problems singly or together. Proper tire balance provides the smoothest riding comfort and keeps wear to a minimum. Out-of-balance tires can cause very disturbing vehicle vibration, especially at freeway speeds. Unbalanced tires can result in "feathering," a graduated wear pattern that goes from bad to worse. *Cupping*, where small bits of rubber are gouged, and *flat spots*, are other possible problems caused by unbalanced tires. Once wear patterns like these begin they only get worse; a balance at this stage will not correct the problem nor slow the wear process. The profile of the tire has already been destroyed.

---

## HINT

*Tire chains excel in the areas of balancing and alignment. Tire stores do more than any other repair facility because in one shop they might do dozens of alignments whereas other facilities manage only a few. Why are they experts in alignment and balance? To protect their tires, of course! An improperly aligned or balanced tire will lead to tire failure, which leads to a free (for the customer) yet costly (for the chain) tire replacement. Therefore, it is in their best interest for you to get the best wear and mileage out of their tires.*

---

Balance is fairly inexpensive, but if you're purchasing new tires, the purchase price should include balancing. The tires themselves could cost hundreds of dollars, and many tire chains like to charge $3.00 to $6.00 per tire additional to spin balance them. Many people just accept that as a necessary evil and pay the price. But if you indicate that you won't purchase the tires unless the balance is included, it is likely the tire store will yield and throw in balancing for free. They can't afford to lose the sale of new tires at a price of hundreds of dollars for $25.00 worth of balancing, especially when their competitor down the street might be offering the service for free. Balancing is an expendable item for most tire stores.

Some people believe that rear tires do not have to be balanced, and it is true that the rear tires are not subject to the vibration, stress and load the front tires are, but it is not wise to believe this analogy. When all tires come out of the factory mold none of them are perfectly round.

Some can be off only fractions of an ounce while others might take two or three ounces to put them right. But if I were to see a tire mechanic adding more than three ounces to a brand new tire I would stop him and ask him to try another new tire. Such heavy counter-weights when used on a new passenger tire could be an indication of a deformity in the tire mold and that the tire is warped. Large multiple-ply truck tires might take much more weight to balance them but the same rule applies to them as well; too much weight needed would indicate a problem. You can generally assume that the less balancing weight a tire requires the better its profile and mold distribution are.

**Valve Stems**—Valve stems are usually replaced along with new tires, because their life is usually as long. However, like balancing, stems should be included in the purchase price, although the unsuspecting customer is often charged for them.

## WARRANTY/GUARANTEE

Many people don't realize that when they purchase new tires they usually receive a warranty or guarantee. Some tire invoices state the seller will repair, inspect and rotate your tires periodically at no charge. If you pick up a bolt or a nail in one of your tires, the shop where you purchased it is likely to fix it on the spot. This amenity can save you around $10. Even if you have caught that nail miles away there is a good chance that you can make it to the shop that sold it to you. The same goes for a tire rotation. This can be a free and regular service which lets them worry about the condition of your tires instead of you.

Be sure to read and save your tire contracts. Quite often these guarantees are hidden in the fine print, and they are not always brought to your attention when you purchase the tires.

## SCARE TACTICS

Because tires are so critical to safety, a repair customer is vulnerable to several scare tactics used by tire chains to convince them to buy. Some are subtle, some not so. I know of a service manager who liked to take a regular 8-1/2 x 11-inch sheet of note paper and let it drop to the floor of a customer's feet. He would then point out that it represented the contact area between his tire and the road surface. He would go on to say that it was the difference between safety and plummeting off a cliff on a wet, slick mountain road.

More subtle is the TV advertising campaign of a major international tire manufacturer that features a tiny, near-naked baby who glides across your TV set on a tire, giggling and laughing, with the narrator saying "When so much is riding on your tires. . ." Images of a tire blowout at speed, or of your car veering out of control toward an oncoming truck with the kids squabbling in the back seat dance through your mind. Within seconds, you're signing the repair invoice and plunking down the cash for the best tires money can buy.

To be sure, there are obvious reasons why a tire should be replaced. If a chunk of tread is missing, if the steel belt is poking through the tread, if the sidewalls are cracked and weathered, if the tire is almost bald. . . these are all obvious indications that a new tire is indeed necessary. But don't be scared into purchasing a more expensive tire, or one that isn't needed. Use your own judgment. If you are not a performance driver, don't be sold performance tires.

## ALIGNMENT

Alignment is a catchall word that covers the many adjustments of your car's front suspension. If you really get into it, you'll find the science behind it baffling, concerned with technical geometric theory and formulas. And because of this complexity, many people are easily led to believe by shady mechanics that if they'll just pay for a $70 alignment, then the mysterious vibration or pull will disappear. Quite often, the same problems could be remedied by simply inflating the tires properly or by having a tire balanced (around $10). Let's see if we can't make this mysterious alignment business a little less complicated.

## SELF-DIAGNOSIS

Your car's alignment can be knocked out of whack if you were to hit a deep pothole hard, or smack curb while attempting a difficult parallel parking maneuver. Or, the adjustments can simply come loose with vehicle age. Improper alignment will call attention to itself with a vibration felt through the steering wheel, or, your car may drift to the left or right rather than follow a straight line if you should let go of the steering wheel momentarily. Your tires could also be wearing unevenly, faster on one side than the other.

**Other Causes**—But before you rush off to the nearest alignment rack, rule out some other possibilities first. Check the tire pressures to make sure they are all set to the recommended setting. Check to make sure all wheel weights used to balance the tires are in place. If you can't find them, then be sure to ask the tire store to check for them and rule out that possibilty.

What are the exceptions when dealing with a pull? When the pull is not that noticeable, yet the car still turns either way from its straight and intended course, it is called a *drift*. It could be a slight drift in which the car eventually ends up to the left or right after a while. You might notice a pull in a hundred or so feet of driving whereas in the case of a drift or slight drift it might take you a quarter of a mile to notice it. Both a pull and a drift can be the result of an improper caster setting.

What else could make your car pull or drift? A damaged front end suspension part would. What if you had a grossly underinflated tire on your left front? Since we know that more air in a tire causes it to roll easier we can assume that an underinflated tire would drag. If that front tire was low and dragging it would pull or make the car drift in that direction. A car will pull or drift to the side of a wheel that has its brakes dragging (not to be confused with a brake pull, which happens when the pedal is applied). A car will pull or drift if one of the front tires is damaged, worn or deformed in some way. And certainly a car will drift on a "crowned" road; because some roads are built higher in the middle to assist with water drainage. Since you drive on the right side of the road you can expect that the road will canter to the right or toward the rain gutter. Thus your car might move slightly in this direction while driving.

## UNDERSTANDING THE LINGO

Many mechanics will fire a barrage of technical terms your way to confuse and intimidate you into having an alignment done, and to impress upon you that great technical expertise is required and the high charge is justified. The truth be told, the mechanic probably knows about as much as you will after reading about the following terms, more than likely he will know less! Most of the guesswork in alignment is taken care of by a sophisticated alignment rack that can be easily operated. So a quick briefing on the related terms can be to your advantage. These terms can be easily understood if you just think of your feet as the front tires of your car.

**Toe**—If you have to, go out and stand directly in front of your car with your back to the front bumper. With your feet set slightly apart, in a normal stance, point your toes slightly outward. Now imagine that your front tires have just done the same thing; both of them pointing outwards (away from each other), just like your toes are. Now bring your toes back to pointing straight ahead. Now, point your toes inward as though you were assuming a knock-kneed stance and imagine, behind you, that your tires have just done the same thing. Come back to your straight stance.

When your tires are toed inward (knock-kneed) it is called *negative toe-in*. One tire can be straight (call that zero degrees) and the other tire can be pointing inward (negative-negative degrees). Just remember that zero degrees or very close to it (toes pointing straight ahead) represents normal in the case of your tires.

Pointing your toes outward (bow-legged) is *positive toe-out*, or they are toed-out. Out = positive. In = negative. Similarly, you can have one tire positive and the other tire normal (straight ahead). You could have one tire positive and the other one negative. Sort of a half bow-legged half knock-kneed situation. You can even turn around facing your car and do this; you will get the same effect.

Get it? You've just learned a very important measurement that the mechanic has to make. He wants to point your tires straight down the road (or whatever the specification book says—some manufacturers like your car to go down the road with slightly negative toe). But for our purpose just remember that straight is great.

---

## HINT

*Many new cars today no longer need the camber and caster alignment adjustment. The front end parts are pre-set with no allowable tolerance. If you do discover from a mechanic that you have a caster or camber problem and that there is no adjustment for it on your car, be prepared to pay for a new part to remedy the problem. How can one of these parts go wrong in the first place? They can be worn or damaged by hard and erratic driving habits. Sometimes, striking a steep and sharp curve at moderate speed can bend a front end component.*

---

How can you tell if your tires are negative or positive toe? It's kind of hard without the alignment rack but there is a way to look for it in tire wear. If a tire is pointed inward too much (negative toe) it will have a "feathered" wear on the inside of the tire. If a tire is pointed too far outward (positive toe), it will wear on the outside of the tire and only there.

**Camber**—Things start to get a little more confusing because camber can wear your tires just like a negative or positive toe problem. In fact, camber is responsible for wearing your tires on the inside and outside more than toe does. Could you have a toe problem and a camber problem at the same time? Yes. Let's go back to the front of the car again. Keep your feet planted flat, then roll your feet so you are standing on the outsides. Visualize if you can that the tire is now riding more on its outside surface than it is on its inside surface. It's kind of tilted on its edge, isn't it? Now if it were to ride like that it would certainly wear out the outside edge of the tire because it's tilted—the tire is not seated flat on the ground. Since it is going to wear the outside edge of the tire it is going to have positive camber wear (just like a toed-out condition would produce positive toe or positive wear). Now roll your feet inward so you are standing on the insides of your feet. This is called negative camber and it would wear the inside of the tire.

Now straighten up and stand normally. Like toe, this is the normal position for your tire to rest on—flat on the ground. This camber measurement is in degrees as well. Can you have one tire with positive camber and the other one negative? Yes, because each wheel has a separate adjustment—most cars are equipped with independent front suspension. It is also conceivable that you could have a negative toe and a negative camber on one tire. If these adjustments were large you could really have a heck of a worn tire.

**Caster**—There is one more adjustment that you should be familiar with. There is no need to explain the adjustment or position of the tire in this case since it does not normally wear tires like toe and camber. It is called *caster*. More than anything else (with a few exceptions) an improper caster setting will be responsible for a pull to the left or right while you are driving down a straight and level road. If your car pulls to the left the mechanic makes an adjustment that offsets this discrepancy. The idea is to get your car back into a position where it tracks straight. Caster is normally associated with a noticeable or even a hard pull to either direction. Just remember that caster pulls.

✔ The L.O.F. (lube, oil, filter) is the most important and frequent preventative maintenance chore a vehicle operator performs.

✔ Oil breaks down and loses its viscosity (thickness). It should be changed (along with the filter) in accordance with the manufacturer's recommendations. When it's black as night, it's time for a change.

✔ Determine which brand, weight and quality oil your vehicle uses by consulting your owner's manual. Not all oils are alike. Some can increase fuel economy, some are used in hotter and colder temperatures, etc.

✔ Use quality brand name engine oils like, Quaker State, Pennzoil, Havoline, Valvoline, etc.

✔ Use quality replacement filters like, Fram, AC-Delco, Motorcraft, Pennzoil and STP.

✔ All front-end and chassis parts should be lubricated with an L.O.F. service. This includes the upper and lower control arm bushings, all ball joints, tie rod ends, idler arm, U-joints, Pitman arm and any other component that is equipped with a zerk fitting.

✔ Make sure the mechanic installs the new "O" ring or gasket supplied with the new filter. The oil filter should be hand tightened only. Also, make sure that the filler cap and dipstick have been replaced after the service. The hectic pace in quick stop facilities breeds this type of careless mistake.

✔ All fluid reservoirs should be checked and appropriately filled as part of the L.O.F service. This includes the: rear end oil, automatic transmission, gear box (standard transmission), power steering fluid, brake fluid, radiator or reservoir (water), battery water and even the windshield washer reservoir! Make sure the special "23-point" service includes refills. Define the difference between check and refill with the L.O.F. place.

✔ Generally, tires with less than 2/32 of an inch, or tires that have worn through the tread bars, should be replaced.

✔ Tires should always be replaced with a similar size, design and make. Don't mix tire makes. They come in bias, bias-belted and radial designs.

✔ Avoid purchasing re-cap tires unless you prefer this inexpensive substitute. They don't carry the same warranty/guarantee packages that new original tires do. They are prone to premature failure, often without warning.

✔ Tire inflation is very important and can affect safety, wear, fuel economy and handling. Consult your owner's manual for proper inflation pressures. Check tire pressure at least every 45 days, or when you plan to change the load factor or take a trip. Pocket tire gauges are available at parts stores.

✔ Tire rotation prolongs tire life. Radials are typically rotated from back to front. Crossing radial tires can result in a "radial pull," which is a twist or flex in the fabric of the tire. Rotate every six to ten thousand miles. Rotation is sometimes a free service included with the purchase of new tires—so is puncture damage and inspection. Be sure to take advantage of it.

✔ Remember that if a tire requires too many weights (ounces) to balance properly, it could be an indication of a deformity in the tire mold. The better tires require only one or two ounces of counterweight.

✔ Proper alignment can deter serious tire wear. A car that is not aligned properly can cause the car to pull left or right of its intended straight course.

✔ Always have your tires properly inflated before having your car aligned. A pull does not always mean that your car is out of alignment. Front tires that are under or overinflated can easily cause a pull. A pull can also be the cause of a defective radial tire (radial pull or twist). Also, check tire balance if you feel a steering vibration.

✔ Insist that a mechanic perform all of the necessary adjustments on your car when he aligns it. Have him note the adjustments made on the repair order. Many times, they'll think you don't know the difference and set just one area and not the rest. Make sure the invoice lists toe, camber and caster checks and adjustments.

✔ Buying new tires does not mean that you must always align your car, although since many tire chains are willing to throw this service in for free, it's a good idea. However, if your old tires were wearing evenly, you can assume that your car is still in proper alignment.

✔ Save your receipt or tire warranty/guarantee certificate. File it away in a safe place and always bring it with you to the original store (or sister store) when you want your new tires checked out, repaired, pro-rate adjusted, or rotated. Many warranty/guarantee packages include free road hazard and puncture service. Take advantage of every amenity they offer you with new tires and related services.

# 5

# EXHAUST SYSTEMS

## THE INS & OUTS OF MUFFLER REPAIR

There are more components to the exhaust system than just the muffler, a fact many people don't realize. When confronted with a simple muffler exchange, the muffler mechanic might start talking about CATs, air injection systems, hydrocarbons and the like until your head spins.

Most exhaust systems are durable and can last up to 70,000 miles, or in some cases up to 100,000 miles, depending on the climate of the area you live in. Rain, snow, road salt and sea air salt can be determining factors as to how long the system will last.

## EXHAUST COMPONENTS

### THE EXHAUST MANIFOLD

The exhaust manifold bolts directly to the cylinder head. If your car has two cylinder heads (as in the case of a V8 or V6 engine) it will have two exhaust manifolds. A manifold is sealed to the cylinder head with a gasket, studs and nuts. Its function is to draw hot exhaust gas from the head (s) and into the front exhaust pipe where it is routed through the catalytic converter, the muffler, then out the rear tailpipe where it makes a contribution to smog and the impending "Greenhouse" effect.

**Common Problems**—Some manifolds work in conjunction with a thermostatically controlled air cleaner. You can tell this by the appearance of a cowl or metal housing that wraps around the exhaust manifold. From this a flexible, aluminum coated hose is directed up from the manifold and secured into the bottom of the air cleaner snorkel. The prime function of this system is to increase the temperature of the intake air to the carburetor during warm-up. The hotter air helps vaporize the raw unburned fuel and provides a better air/fuel mixture for total combustion. This hot air is drawn up when the engine is first started—this helps the engine warm up faster and burn away any unburned fuel. Quite often, this flexible hose will tear, affecting the cold-starting capability of your car. Due to a choke system automobiles always burn a richer mixture of fuel during cold start. And this is when toxic emissions are most prevalent. This is an important point to remember during a smog check. For more on that turn to chapter 10.

There is not too much that can go wrong with an exhaust manifold. Between the cylinder head and the manifold is a gasket. This gasket can leak, which would result in a loss of exhaust efficiency, decreased power and an increase in fuel mileage. Sometimes exhaust manifolds crack which causes loud under-the-hood exhaust noise and often exhaust fumes. Replacing a cracked exhaust manifold might be a warranty item. If not, it's expensive. In fact, replacing the manifold gasket is also very expensive. Not because the gasket costs much. It doesn't. But the amount of time required to get at the gasket is quite high, and when it comes to auto repair, time is money.

## THE EXHAUST PIPE

The exhaust pipe is generally maintenance-free. It is constructed of heavy gauge steel and is designed with the least amount of bends and constrictions to aid in the free flow of escaping exhaust gas. The pipe is typically supported by several shock-type mounting brackets. On many new vehicles the pipe is one continuous piece, with the muffler welded between the front and tail section. On vehicles equipped with emission control the catalytic converter is clamped into place to facilitate its ease of removal and replacement.

Exhaust pipes will suffer rot, rust and deterioration in conditions of snow, ice and heavy rainfall. Salt, when used to deter icy conditions on roads, has adverse effects on the complete exhaust system metal. Exhaust pipes and systems are equally subject to impact damage when vehicles hit low spots or obstructions. Furthermore, the hangers that hold them in place can become loose, especially rubber hangers, which causes the exhaust pipe to vibrate. Excessive and constant vibration can cause the pipe to crack at the weld seams.

Complete exhaust pipes, from the manifold on back, can be quite expensive when purchased from a dealer. As stated before, the exhaust pipe and muffler are often welded together as one unit, but quite often a muffler chain won't have that single piece. What they do have is a multi-piece system and if that's the way you go, expect to pay much more than the advertised special.

## THE CAT

The CAT, or catalytic converter, is the central component to an emission control system. The catalytic converter is an insulated stainless-steel container within the exhaust system resembling a conventional exhaust muffler. Exhaust gases passing through the converter are chemically neutralized by one or more activating catalysts. These catalysts, consisting of platinum and palladium, are used to speed up the burning of excess hydrocarbons and carbon monoxide, producing harmless carbon dioxide and water.

So, in essence, a catalytic converter is a chemical tank that serves as an afterburner to reduce harmful emissions. The extremely high temperatures that occur in the converter also help to burn off unburned fuel, HC and CO.

**Common Problems**—I've seen stickers on new cars with warnings from the manufacturer stating that you must take care not to drive your car when the engine is malfunctioning in order to avoid damage to the CAT. I have only seen one case where a converter was noticeably damaged by an engine miss. And this vehicle was supposedly driven with a major engine malfunction for over a year in that condition. The outside appearance of the converter was noticeably burned, exuding a "rotten egg" smell. The metal skin of the converter, in particular the top and sides, gave the appearance of a bluish rainbow effect— evidence of extreme temperatures. It is safe to assume that this converter was damaged internally and would have to be replaced. But I think that the hype that has been printed about the precautions concerning the catalytic converter are, at best, extreme.

According to the MVPC (Motor Vehicle Pollution Control) Handbook for installation and inspection stations: "There is no universal field test method for inspecting converters at this time." The California Bureau of Automotive Repair recommends that you follow the vehicle manufacturer's procedure, which varies from car to car.

In an effort to learn more about the newest technology concerning the catalytic converter I contacted Mr. Duane Bilderback, an emission control engineer at the California Bureau Of Automotive Repair. It was his contention that there was really no surefire way to diagnose a faulty converter but they did have some new ideas lined up. "Most complaints with the catalytic converter have been symptomatic and imagined," he went on to say.

So what does all this mean? It means that no one seems to be able to agree when the catalytic converter is bad. If you suspect it is bad, or are told as much, then go immediately to your dealership. For more on that, see *Shams*, page 76.

## MUFFLERS

Mufflers are a more simplified version of the converter. Like the catalytic converter they are constructed of heavy gauge steel, wrapped in a tank-like canister.

They are usually located behind the converter and attach inline with the exhaust pipe. They do not have any catalyst material inside. Instead they contain interior steel baffles and plates. These baffles are constructed and situated within the muffler to slow down and interrupt the exhaust flow, thus suppressing noise and arresting spark or hot particles.

That is a muffler's chief purpose; to suppress excess noise and arrest spark. On many new factory cars, the stock muffler is often welded directly to the exhaust pipe. This probably cuts down on labor time and negates the use of clamps, which could be very costly when there are thousands of cars produced. When that stock muffler is replaced by one other than a stock unit from the vehicle manufactuer, it is torched, or cut off with a pipe cutter. Then a new muffler is usually installed with small adapter pipes and U-bolt clamps. From then on, if it requires another muffler it can be easily bolted into place.

**Resonators**—Resonators are made of the same material as converters and mufflers. They might be slightly smaller than mufflers and appear more cylindrical in shape. They are often located behind the muffler somewhere near the rear of the vehicle in proximity to the tail pipe.

Resonators are really secondary mufflers. Years ago they were used often on the large full-sized luxury cars such as Cadillacs and Lincolns. Still in existence today, resonators serve the purpose as an additional suppression device to further reduce exhaust noise to a minimum.

Resonators might cost more than mufflers because most repair shops, aside from the muffler chains, do not stock them. Often they are a special order part and are difficult to find. It is ironic that a resonator, a secondary or backup system to the muffler, can cost two or three times as much as a muffler. A vehicle with dual exhaust (two mufflers and two resonators), can get quite expensive when it comes to replacing the entire exhaust system.

**Common Problems**—It doesn't take a test pilot to figure out when the muffler needs to be replaced, unless of course you're hard of hearing, in which case passing motorists, the police, or angry neighbors will let you know that it's time. Mufflers are subject to rust, rain, salt, humidity, sleet and snow, as well as vibration. These are all factors that can lead to deterioration.

# HARDWARE

Hardware refers to all of the accessory items used to secure the exhaust system to the car. The stock system on your car may not have all of these components, but they are commonly used by large muffler chains to replace stock systems with their own generic kind. So if you go to a large muffler chain, for example, you might have to pay for some of these additional items so they can install their system on your car. More on this in a moment. First, let's find out what the hardware is.

**Hangers**—Hangers are mounting hardware used to secure the exhaust pipe to the underneath of the car. They come in a variety of shapes and sizes for different make automobiles. Most of them have rubber or fabric shock-type bands that absorb vibration and are designed to give when under stress and load. Many Toyotas, for example, have a rubber band connector that allows the exhaust system to move and shift when subject to heavy shock and vibration. Most hangers are stocked by the large muffler shops. Some foreign vehicle hangers can be ordered only via a dealership.

The important thing to remember about hangers is that they should be periodically checked to see that the mounting brackets are tight and that the fabric or rubber shock connectors are not worn, torn, or weathered. A $10.00 hanger that breaks at the connector can allow the exhaust system to sag in one spot, thus creating a condition where it might catch on speed bumps, curves or other obstacles. Even at a moderate speed a sagging muffler can catch on an obstruction and be torn away from the exhaust pipe.

**Adapters**—Muffler adapters are used to adapt a replacement muffler to the diameter of your exhaust pipe. They are about six inches long and come in various widths. Typically, two adapters are used on each muffler; one in the front and one in the rear.

They are made of the same material as the exhaust pipe and are usually supplied along with a muffler package.

**Clamps**—Muffler clamps are those U-bolts that you see that make the tight connection between the muffler and the adapter. They come in various sizes depending upon the diameter of the adapter and muffler connecting pipe.

Some familiar sizes are: 1-1/2-, 1-3/4-, 2-, 2-1/4- and 2-1/2-inch diameters. Clamps are normally part of a new muffler package unless you buy them separately. In most cases clamps and adapters are provided free with a new muffler—but not hangers and the brackets. You can expect to pay for them as an additional service part.

I would seriously question the policy of a muffler shop that charged extra for adapters and clamps with a new muffler installation. In any advertisement I would look for the words "complete muffler, $19.95, installed." That means that they are required to furnish the parts to make their new muffler fit your car—adapters and clamps. I would not pay the additional and separate price for these parts with a "muffler special."

## SHAMS

Mufflers are one of the most common R & R items, and shops like this type of work because the profit margin is high. There are a couple of scenarios that you will have to be on the lookout for when approached by a mechanic or manager who informs you that you need a new muffler system.

**Lifetime Warranty**—Some of the larger chains will offer a "lifetime warranty" on the new muffler, or for as long as you own your car. This sounds like a deal too good to be true and it is. A few years later, you'll come in to get the free muffler, and you could end up paying more than you did the first time. Sure, the replacement muffler will be free, but you'll be charged premium prices for the pipes, labor, gaskets and the cost of torching. Second, if your first muffler lasted for 70,000 miles, will you still own the car for another 70,000 miles? The additional cost of a lifetime warranty may not be necessary.

**The CAT Scam**—I've heard too many stories of folks who have been told their car won't pass a smog inspection because they needed a new, and very expensive, catalytic converter. Many of these same folks went ahead and paid the price, because in some states, a smog certification is mandatory (more on this in chapter 10).

Many owners will be shown a rusted catalytic converter and told "it's rotted out, so you'll need to replace it." There are a couple of things wrong with this. More often than not, the rust will only be on the surface and the rest of the metal will be fine. But second, most parts related to emissions, such as the CAT, fuel injection, manifolds, etc., are covered under a 5-year, 50,000 mile manufacturer's warranty. Why? Because the federal government makes it so. So if you're told that the CAT needs to be replaced, don't plunk down upwards of $500. Go to the dealer and have him check it out and if it needs to be replaced, it should be covered under warranty—provided the car is within the limit stated above.

**The Rattle**—Let's say, for instance, that you pull into a service center for an oil change. You sign an invoice (for an L.O.F. only) then take a seat in the waiting room. Moments later you are summoned to the garage and a mechanic is waiting under your car, which has been placed on a hydraulic lift. He has the wheels off your vehicle and assures you that your brakes look just fine (funny, but you don't remember asking about brakes) but he wants to bring something to your attention. He points to your muffler and, with the bottom of his fist, he gives your muffler a punch. You hear what seems to be pebbles rattling in the muffler.

The mechanic says, "You might want to replace that muffler before it gets any worse." You ask him why and he says, "It's burnt out. The insides are cooked. Hear the metal crashing around in there?"

You're impressed, and want to fix the problem before it gets any worse. Furthermore, you'll be pressured because it will be pointed out to you that the car is already on the lift, and they can get started right away if you'll just sign for it. This is a common scam.

All mufflers on all cars are prone to interior moisture and unburned fuel (cold starts) which causes the insides to rust and corrode. Bits of baffle plate or rust will fall to the bottom of the muffler—not fist-sized chunks, mind you, but small pieces—particles.

The truth is that all mufflers are subject to this condition. It is only when they are internally broken and rotted with large chunks floating about that this diagnosis is correct. In such a state of decay the muffler would certainly be louder. Only you did not have a loud muffler. Just remember that small amounts of rust or decayed particles in your muffler are considered normal and you should not think that your muffler is "burnt out" because it rattles a little on the inside.

**The Rag**—This time the mechanic balls up a shop rag, and while your engine is running, he plugs up your tailpipe stopping the flow of exhaust. He brings your attention to a hissing leak at one of the muffler clamp connections. He tells you that your exhaust is leaking and you should replace the connection. He might even throw in a scare tactic and tell you that dangerous carbon monoxide could leak into the driver's compartment and you wouldn't know it until you passed out. So why don't you spring for a muffler package with new adapters and clamps, a package they just happen to have on sale? Thinking that he is right you okay the repairs. Funny how that hissing noise stopped though when he removed the rag from the tailpipe.

Well let me tell you, any exhaust system will leak *somewhere* if it's force-plugged in this manner. Nine times out of ten it will be a muffler clamp connection that leaks in this fashion. Simply ask the mechanic to tighten the clamp in the vicinity of the leak. Chances are this will solve the problem. In fact, he may have loosened it beforehand.

With time and wear on the exhaust system, clamps and adapters expand and contract with heat. They lose their tensile strength. Exhaust pipe vibration will loosen the nuts on the U-bolt. A little tightening on these parts can remedy moderate exhaust leaks.

**The Torch**—Muffler installers have a habit of torching off your clamps then torch-cutting the adapters loose, because the nuts are usually welded tight with rust. This is fine when skillfully done. However, I have seen dozens of exhaust pipes slit and mutilated in this fashion.

What happens is they torch the adapter sleeve trying to peel it back and inadvertently create a slit in your exhaust pipe. The mistake is easy to cover up because a new adapter covers the slit or burn hole. This is annoying because it can weaken your exhaust pipe at that position, the position where the new clamp must be cinched down. If cinched down too tight, it could crush your weakened pipe. Personally, I would rather see them unbolt and slide these parts off, even if it means snapping the clamp bolt or nut.

Another sham involving torching: some larger chains will charge you for the amount of acetylene used! Now that is a cost I would ask up front about, and refuse to pay.

**Unnecessary Parts**—Muffler shops love to sell you an exhaust pipe along with your muffler. This happens a lot if your muffler is located near the rear of your car. Their explanation is that the muffler and exhaust pipe are welded together, and should be either replaced with a costly one-piece system, or with an even costlier custom, multi-piece system.

The truth is, large muffler chains generally carry the adapters in stock to fit their new muffler with your stock exhaust pipe. All they have to do is cut that weld between the stock exhaust pipe and muffler with a pipe cutter or torch, and install the proper adapter. At worst they might have to reposition your exhaust pipe at that position where it is secured to a hanger after they have done this. Why in heaven's name would you want to buy another exhaust pipe when yours is in perfect working order?

As another example, you might be told that the one-piece stock system is only available at the dealer, but they can add a custom system that includes an exhaust pipe, muffler, hangers, adapters and clamps—a multi-piece system. Though only the muffler is damaged, you'll have to purchase all the other pieces because "it's the only way." Nonsense.

That's how muffler shops make up for their seemingly great "muffler deals." Conceivably, you could drive into a shop for a $19.95 muffler special advertised in the paper, end up paying for four clamps at $6 apiece, two adapters at $10 apiece, and get conned into replacing the pipes on both ends of the muffler for $150. My arithmetic says that muffler special is now about $186 plus tax! Did the shop lose on the muffler special? No. Did you? Probably.

- ✔ The typical exhaust system can last the life of a vehicle and can be considered almost maintenance-free. Mufflers, resonators and exhaust pipes suffer wear and deterioration more frequently than the other parts.

- ✔ A slow engine warm-up might indicate that the hot air pipe on the TAS is not connected securely at the exhaust manifold and the air cleaner snorkel. You can make this visual inspection yourself.

- ✔ Be extremely leery when a mechanic points to your catalytic converter and says that it's "bad." This rush judgment could cost you $500 or more. The likelihood that your CAT is bad, is very unlikely, and would rarely, if ever, cause you to flunk a smog check. Furthermore, if it is bad, it should be covered under warranty. Just tell the mechanic that you'll have the CAT checked by the dealer.

- ✔ Beware of the "rag in the pipe" and the "burned out" diagnosis scenario for mufflers. Exhaust pipe leaks (at the clamp positions) are sometimes mistaken for faulty mufflers. All mufflers accumulate a moderate amount of rust that falls to the bottom of the muffler canister. Severe breakage of the baffle plates, or excessive noise, would be legitimate reasons for replacing a muffler, but not a little rattle.

- ✔ If your muffler is considered a "one-piece" assembly, and the mechanic says that it must accompany a new exhaust pipe, challenge him and ask him to use adapters to fit a new muffler to your old exhaust pipe.

- ✔ Remember that clamps and adapters should come with a new muffler package. Question anyone who wants to charge you additionally for these parts. Hangers (mounting brackets) are an exception. They cost extra and many times have to come from a dealership.

✔ If your old muffler is "torched" off your vehicle, make sure that they do not cut or mutilate your exhaust pipe in the process, nor that you are charged for acetylene waste.

✔ It is very common for a muffler or resonator to carry a lifetime guarantee. Make sure that you receive your guarantee certificate and file it in a safe place. Slight leaks often occur after your exhaust system has been worked on. This comes from heat expansion and vibration and it could be a week or month after you have had the work done. Your guarantee and invoice is necessary in order to return to the shop and have the problem solved at "N/C" (no charge) to you. Any peculiar noise, rattles or thumps as a result of a misaligned exhaust pipe, hanger, or muffler fitting can also be taken care of at this time.

# 6

# BRAKES

## STOP IF YOU CAN, THEN PROCEED WITH CAUTION

Brakes are one of the most frequently performed repair jobs in the industry, and they are also one of the most expensive. Most people are stunned into catatonia when they are confronted with the cost of a "standard brake job," which normally runs into the hundreds of dollars. This area of repair is also one of the most profitable for a repair shop, and because of the related safety factors and numerous parts to a complete brake job, it's prone to plenty of shams and scams.

## THE STANDARD BRAKE JOB

In many cases a standard brake job just isn't standard anymore. You are getting less for that advertised special and paying more for unnecessary parts and services. The primary reason is that brake jobs represent a tremendous bonus ticket (to the shops that sponsor bonuses) for the mechanic. Brake work is performed more often than exhaust and front end work, and it is only overshadowed by tune-ups and other fast repair. Without question, brake service represents the largest repair ticket in any shop short of major engine work.

The term "safety" rings loud and clear with brake service and every mechanic and service manager knows this too well. Bad brakes on your vehicle immediately conjure up images of accidents, collisions, lawsuits, injuries and other unpleasantries. A vehicle owner is likely to put off other areas of car repair but when it comes to his/her brakes, most people don't mess around. And in a sense that owner is absolutely right—correct in the assumption that good brakes are imperative. But this well known analogy can be taken too far.

Eventually, you will be faced with the realization that you need a standard two- or four-wheel brake job. It can be a disc/drum combination brake job, a four-wheel drum, or a four-wheel disc brake job. It can be a brake job for one axle only, one set, either a front or rear wheel brake job. The important thing is for you to find a facility that can do the job correctly for your vehicle at the best price.

## SELF-DIAGNOSIS

Before I venture into the standard brake inspection let's first examine what you can do to find out if your brakes need to be repaired—before you go marching into a brake shop or authorize a sudden repair because of a flash inspection.

**Pedal Height**—A good determiner is a low brake pedal. Extreme wear of the brake linings would give the brake pedal a lower than normal "feel." With a non-power braking system a noticeably low brake pedal would be more obvious since this pedal would normally ride a bit higher. By low brake pedal I mean a pedal that is to the floor or nearly there. A distance of about 1/2-inch from the floor, when firmly applied, would be cause for alarm. A low brake pedal could denote thin brake lining, adjustment, a low master fluid level, worn drums or rotors, a leak in the brake lines or wheel cylinders, a lack of fluid in the system, bent foot brake linkage, or a combination of any of the above. If the pedal is low, check your master cylinder (located in the engine compartment, usually on the firewall on the driver's side) to make sure the fluid level is up. The problem could be remedied by adding a few ounces of brake fluid, which costs about $3.00 or so.

**Noise**—Brake noise can be associated with any wheel, front or back. It can be defined by a metallic (metal-to-metal) sound—a swish-swish or grating noise, coming directly from the proximity of the affected wheel. This noise is most pronounced when braking for a stoplight or sign, for instance. It frequently resembles a swish sound—this is a result of the rotation of the shoe or pad coming in contact with the drum or rotor. A constant metallic grating (or groan) would indicate that the pad or shoe lining is absent and the surface of the rotor or drum is in direct and constant contact with the shoe or pad backing mount (hard metal). To listen for it accurately, you can drive your car slowly next to a wall, which will amplify the noise.

Actually, to listen for bad brake lining one does not need a "dead silent" environment. Of all the suspicious noises emanating from an automobile, a brake noise is one of the most obvious. It can be quite loud even in city traffic. Sometimes a pad or shoe lining actually breaks away from its mount and causes an audible noise. This happens infrequently but it can still be heard as small clatters or jerky snaps and might be felt in the brake pedal underfoot.

Clicks and rattles may be the result of broken or worn return and hold-down springs—or a broken piece floating inside the drum. For these smaller and less audible noises, such as rattles and clicks coming from the wheels, use the technique of listening while driving against a wall slowly, such as alongside a building. But before you do it remove all the hubcaps on your car if it is so equipped. You would be surprised how many times hub caps pick up pebbles sending them zinging around inside rattling. If you have wire wheel hub caps, check to see that the wire rods are not broken and flopping, causing this noise.

Keep in mind that most brake noise happens when the brakes are applied unless a spring has broken and a shoe is dragging.

Any brake noise, especially the loud swish-swish or grating type, should be taken care of immediately. It means you are metal-to-metal and your ability to stop, especially in a panic situation, is greatly reduced! Brake drums and rotors are extremely expensive, and if you let the problem continue there is a good chance the drum or rotor will be permanently ruined. In many cases, you can only purchase new ones from a dealer, which means paying top dollar.

**Squeals**—Every car made today has front wheel disc brakes. The most common complaint in the noise department is the front wheel brake squeal or squeak. This squeal can be detected in the last stages of braking, and has been known to drive people up the wall.

It is an irritating, loud and inconsistent noise that comes and goes. I've lost count of the number of people who have sworn that they needed new brakes as a result of the disc brake squeal. And I've had to pity the hundreds of customers who went ahead and replaced their brakes because of this problem, or were told as much by shady mechanics. This noise is common and can almost be considered normal. It happens because the brake pads get hot and glazed. The glazed surface of the pad becomes sticky and hangs up, causing this squeal or squeak.

One place I worked for offered a front disc brake "squeal service." It amounted to removing the front wheels, spraying down the pads with a brake cleaning solution, and in some cases sandpapering the pads to knock the glaze off. This "freshened" them up. We charged little for this service, the idea being that the same customer would then come back for a thorough brake job when it was needed—then we'd really sock it to 'em.

Since this service is rather unorthodox I don't expect that it is alive and well today. Mechanics of today like to sell you new pads, and this is just what they'll tell you—"The brake pads are burned or overheated." Well, I've never known any brake pad to stay cool under any condition, but a brake squeal does not mean that your pads are ruined. If you simply cannot stand this squeak or squeal another moment longer, beg your mechanic to knock the glaze off your pads. Let's hope he does, as a favor to you. Give him the money for new pads (a complete front wheel disc brake job) only when the lining is obviously worn, when he shows them to you. Don't fall prey to the "burned" pads theory. Instead, keep a heavy foot off that accelerator and don't ride the brakes from now on.

**Brake Pull**—Brake pull is associated with the front wheels of the vehicle. In most cases it is caused by "contaminated" brake lining. This is a situation where brake fluid has leaked onto the shoe lining or pad via a leaking wheel cylinder or caliper or a defective wheel bearing seal. The fluid or grease makes the contact of the brake lining surface slippery—the pads or shoe lining cannot function by gripping and causing friction. If the leak occurs on one wheel, it won't "grab" as well as the one opposite it, and the car will pull in the direction of the wheel without the fluid. If the pads or shoe lining have been contaminated or wetted it is always advisable to have them replaced and the primary leak traced and repaired.

A worn brake lining or badly scored drums or rotors can also cause brake pull. So can a sticking or defective front caliper piston or wheel cylinder. In the case of front wheel drum brakes, broken hold-down and return springs can interfere with smooth braking operation by binding up or breaking. In any event, a brake pull cries out for immediate attention and an inspection should be performed as soon as possible.

**Soft Pedal**—A soft or "spongy" pedal, a pedal that feels "cushiony" or unfirm when applied, can mean that air is in the brake line system. This happens frequently right after a brake job has been performed. Sometimes a mechanic fails to "bleed" all of the air out of the brake lines. It can be the result of a person who takes one of the wheels off his car and loosens a bleeder nut. When a vehicle owner has to pump up the pedal several times (to get brake height), this can also be the result of air in the brake line system. An empty or near empty master cylinder can cause a sponginess in the pedal or cause the pedal to travel all the way to the floor. Check the fluid in the master cylinder.

**Brake Pulsation**—If you apply your brakes and the pedal "throbs" under your foot, this is known as a "pulsating" pedal. Worn or loose wheel bearings can cause a drum or rotor to rotate sloppily, causing this pulsating condition. Rear axles that are bent or twisted can cause the hub to wobble, and since the hub holds the rear drum in position this leads to its periodic misalignment while rotating.

Drums or rotors that have suffered severe heat damage can become warped or eccentric (out of round). There is a rare condition in which a drum can blister from extreme heat, and just like a boil, it can produce a lump and cause a brake pedal chatter or vibration. Drums and rotors that have suffered this severe heat damage can normally be "cleaned up," or cut smooth on a brake lathe.

Drums and rotors that have become overheated turn a brown or dirty color and give off a noticeable odor. They can become so hot they'll heat up other components, such as rubber wheel cylinder boots and cups, grease and even the brake pads and lining, which are made out of asbestos materials. Braking your vehicle hard while towing heavy loads downhill, leaving the emergency brake on a few notches and hard-driving habits—all contribute to overheating brake conditions. With extreme heat comes metal and component warpage, thus causing a part to be misaligned.

**Brake Drag**—Brake drag is a condition in which your brakes do not release fully after depressing the pedal. This can be the result of a broken hold-down or return spring. A sticking by-pass port in a master cylinder can cause this condition and lead to the brakes dragging.

Sticking pistons inside the caliper or wheel cylinder can freeze up in a braking position and cause constant friction and contact. One of the most common problems associated with brake drag has been when a vehicle owner leaves the emergency brake on in a position where it actuates the shoes against the drums. Of course, if a mechanic has adjusted the rear brakes too tightly, this can cause them to drag— which builds up heat, causing them to expand and drag further.

A condition of hot and dragging brakes is a serious one that can lead to enormous expense. You can tell your brakes are dragging because you'll often smell it. The smell is an acrid, sharp odor. If you pull over you might spot smoke coming out from the affected wheel. If a vehicle is operated with dragging brakes for a time sufficient to put strain on the engine, it is entirely likely that the automatic transmission could suffer major component damage. Transmission clutches could burn, and delicate seals could burst causing an immediate loss of transmission fluid. If you experience this condition while on a trip or far away from a service center, pull over, stop and seek immediate repair assistance. If no assistance is available it is wise to let the brakes cool off before proceeding any further.

**Fluid Level**—Any time the brake master cylinder fluid is low, or nearly empty, fill it up. If it drains quickly, it is time to inspect the condition of the wheel cylinders, calipers and brake lines, because a sudden and frequent drop in fluid level is an indication that there is a probable leak in the brake system. A preliminary check would be to look at the inside surface of each wheel to spot any fluid leakage. The inside surface of a tire that is soaked or splattered with brake fluid will appear blacker than any other tire.

A master cylinder can develop a leak in the rear seal of the master cylinder body or the line connections to it. A defective rear seal in a master cylinder will show up as a wet spot or stream of fluid against the firewall directly underneath the cylinder body. If this condition is found (low fluid level) in the master cylinder, fill it to its proper capacity and then take the vehicle in for an inspection. If you lose all fluid, then you'll quickly lose your brakes, which can spell disaster. It is unwise to assume that there are no leaks when having to fill or add fluid to the master cylinder.

---

## CAUTION

*Don't let anyone sell you a brake master cylinder because he says it will complement the new brake job he's just sold you, or that it is necessary because you have to do it when the brake pads, shoes and rotors and drums are replaced and machined.*

*A bad master cylinder will produce a brake pedal that goes all the way to the floor with increased and steady foot pressure. They can also be diagnosed as bad when they are leaking from their rear seal—fluid trails down the front of the power assist or down the firewall (not to be mistaken for spilled fluid which gives an almost identical visual symptom). When confronted by this, demand to see the leaking cylinder, and to see evidence of the leak in the master cylinder's area. If the leak is at the wheel or in some brake line elsewhere, there's a good chance the problem is not with the master cylinder.*

---

## INSPECTION

Generally speaking, it takes a tear-down inspection to determine accurately what condition your brake system is in. This means removing the wheels and checking the thickness of the shoes and pads, as well as the thickness, roundness and surface condition of drums and rotors (the "disc"). It should include checking the brake lines, wheel and master cylinders for brake fluid leakage. The hold-down hardware (the small pins and springs that hold your brakes in place) must be visually inspected for strength and reliability. This includes the nails, hold-down and return springs, emergency brake lever, cable sleeve and operating link. Front wheel brake calipers must be examined to determine if the internal pistons are free-moving.

Usually, there is no charge for a brake inspection. In a few shops there could be a minimum shop service charge to determine the fault in the system only: this cost would be in addition to the repairs made. I would avoid a shop that charged for an inspection, there are too many facilities around who will perform this service free of charge.

**Brake Linings**—The first thing a mechanic will inspect is your brake linings—the thickness of the pads or shoes.

Generally, it is time to replace your shoes or pads when you have about 30% or less lining left. This 30% limit seems to be the rule of thumb with used car dealerships because they consider this to be the cut-off line for replacement. Many dealerships have been prosecuted in the past for selling used cars with less than adequate brake lining. Other repair facilities might want to raise that figure to 40% or 50% lining left as the rule to replace brakes. I would choose to put more miles on my brakes rather than have them replaced at the halfway point.

But determining when they need to be replaced can be tricky. A good mechanic can eyeball brake lining and know exactly what percent is left and estimate how many more miles they will last. He could very well examine your set of brakes and know that you have 50% lining left but he could say 30% is left. And how would you know? You can demand that he give you a side-by-side comparison of your worn brake pad or shoe and a new one. Then you can eyeball it yourself.

Also, remember that during inspection, the mechanic will look for the wheel with the most worn lining and base his percentage judgment on that wheel. You could have 60% lining left on three wheels and 30% lining on one wheel, yet he will pass judgment on that bad wheel and

---

## CAUTION

*So what if the mechanic shows you that the left front pad is worn, the right pad is okay, and the rear shoes are okay, but he says you have to have a four-wheel brake job because you can't have some new pads/shoes and some old ones? He's half right. You should recondition your brakes in axle sets. In other words, in the above example, both front brake pads should be replaced even though one is okay. However, if the rear shoes are fine, then they don't need to be changed at all. The same could be said if the fronts were fine, but the one rear shoe was worn. You can leave the fronts alone, but must change both rears. Don't fall for the scam of "you must always recondition and replace all four brakes at the same time." The front brakes on front-engined cars wear out almost 2 times faster than the rears.*

recommend that you purchase a complete brake job. In a case like this, you would only need to replace the axle set with the 30% lining, but not the other axle set (see the sidebar on p. 87).

Many new cars have an electronic sensor that warns the owner of a brake lining deficiency via a dash light. These type of brakes come with a sensor wire embedded in the pads and when the lining wears to a certain point the information is relayed to the driver.

**Disc Brake Pads**—Most all cars have disc brakes in the front, some have them in the rear as well. The proximity of the pad mounting plate in relation to the rotor is the distance that determines the thickness of the lining. The asbestos pad on disc brakes wears in direct proportion to its use and age. A normal new disc brake pad is about 1/2-inch thick. When it approaches a thickness of about 1/8 inch it is near to replacement—or obviously when it is completely gone—causing a metal-to-metal condition. The mechanic will also advise that you replace your brake lining if it has become contaminated or wetted by brake fluid or bearing grease. Contamination means that the fluid or grease has permeated the porous material of the brake lining, rendering it ineffective. Once they are soaked they have lost their true ability to cause adequate friction. So in a sense, just a small amount of fluid on one pad could cost you a two-wheel brake job. Old brake fluid also has a habit of deteriorating some fibers and materials with which it comes in contact.

**Drum Shoes**—If your car is equipped with drum brakes (the majority of cars today are equipped with front disc/rear drum brake systems, although many performance-oriented and some upmarket cars are equipped with 4-wheel disc brakes), then the rear brake shoes need to be checked. They are inspected in the same manner as the front disc brake pads—with the rear wheels and drums off. The relative thickness of the lining on both shoes, on either wheel, determines their condition. Since drum brake shoes are larger (more surface area) they are not as thick as disc brake pads when new. When new, they are approximately 3/8 of an inch in thickness and can wear until they are paper thin before contacting the metal rivets that hold them on the shoe frame. When it wears to the rivets, shoe lining will always make a metal-to-metal noise. Any shiny metal surface on a brake shoe indicates that it is worn beyond its capacity to function.

**Wheel Cylinder**—In addition to checking the pads and shoes a mechanic should also look for a leaking wheel cylinder. The wheel cylinder (in the case of drum brakes) is located near the top of the backing plate and bolted to it. It is similar in size to a "D" type battery. Inside the cylinder are two cups and two pistons. It is the piston's job to expand the brake shoes so they make contact with the drum. The pistons are forced outward by a surge of brake fluid when the brake pedal is applied. The cups inside the cylinder are responsible for keeping the brake fluid within, acting as a seal or retainer. Once these cups have worn from repeated action they lose their elasticity and allow brake fluid to pass by, through the dust boots on the end of the cylinder body and onto the brake lining and parts. A mechanic has only to remove a dust boot to see if the interior of the cylinder edge is wet. If it shows just the slightest amount of moisture he will recommend that it be replaced or rebuilt. A typical cylinder rebuilding kit will contain two new dust boots, two cups and a new return spring (the spring is located between the pistons).

**Calipers**—The mechanic should also check the condition of the calipers. The calipers are what "squeeze" the brake pads onto the rotor when the brake pedal is applied. They have a cylinder with one large piston in it (some exotic sports cars have more than one piston). An "O" ring seals the piston to the caliper housing. Like a wheel cylinder, the caliper has a dust boot that can be pulled back to check for internal leakage. A caliper is rebuilt much the same way as a wheel cylinder, only there are no cups, just an "O" ring and a new dust boot per wheel.

**Rebuilding Calipers & Cylinders**—Find a shop that includes this service in their brake package. Insist, if necessary, that it be performed, or better yet, stand within visual distance and make sure that it is! About the only legitimate excuse a mechanic can have for replacing your wheel cylinder (not rebuilding it) is if the inside of the cylinder body is pitted and scored from age and dirty brake fluid. The inside of

---

## CAUTION

*Wheel cylinders and calipers are parts often pushed onto an unsuspecting customer. Few people realize they can be rebuilt at a substantial savings over new items. If the seals are leaking, don't be pressured into purchasing new ones by a mechanic who insists they can't be rebuilt. If he finds a leaking wheel cylinder he is apt to sell you not one, but a whole set. Why? Because they bolt on very quickly—the profit margin is higher, and you'll probably go for it after they scare you with "you don't want to take a chance on brakes."*

*In the case of rebuilding a caliper, sure, it's a hassle, and it's a hassle that he'd like to avoid. Even when this service has been included in the standard advertised brake job, I've seen mechanics smear oil over the dust boots to give the impression that it has been done. Especially the caliper rebuilding. It takes awhile to get a new seal around that piston and back in the caliper housing. Calipers require additional tear-down time.*

the cylinder body can always be honed out to clean rust and grime away. But if the metal bore surface is pitted and eaten, it will not seal with new cups; therefore it should be replaced.

**Measuring Drums & Rotors**—The next inspection the mechanic will make will be very important. He should, if he has been trained properly, use an inside micrometer (that is preset to the drum diameter) to measure how much surface material is left on the inside of the brake drums. It is a measurement that denotes the inside diameter of the drum and is usually expressed in thousands of an inch, i.e., .060 or .090. An outside micrometer is used to check the thickness of the rotor because it is a disc and must be measured externally. If the drums or rotors are to be machined, there must be enough material left to machine out scores and pits and still remain within the minimum tolerance.

The minimum tolerances are specified by the manufacturer. If, for instance, a drum diameter exceeds that allowed by the manufacturer, it must be replaced because policy and law dictate this. That is why it is important for a mechanic to actually use the gauges to make these accurate and critical measurements. Just one false reading on one drum or rotor could mean the difference of $90.00 on your repair bill. Too many mechanics want to eyeball these parts and make snap decisions on their appearance alone. For example, a drum can look terribly chewed up and scored on its inside surface but miraculously it can "mic out" and fall within manufacturers specifications, particularly if the vehicle is new. Many drums and rotors that have been scored will clean up after several cuts on the brake lathe.

If you are told that you need a new drum or a new rotor, the mechanic or manager is obligated to prove it to you by revealing the measurement, and recording it on your invoice as further testimony. If in doubt about the condition of one of your rotors or drums, ask for this proof of service and legitimacy. If they say that the wear exceeds the minimum tolerance, ask to see the written tolerance specifications in their manual. If they refuse, then you are probably being scammed. Go somewhere else.

# BRAKE PARTS

**Shoes & Pads**—If you've been convinced that the brake shoes & pads (linings) have been honestly inspected and you agree they are worn, you'll have to choose what type you want. If the mechanic doesn't ask, you should ask what type they are. The two most popular types of brake linings are the asbestos type and the metallic type. Metallic brake shoes have small bits of metal molded into the shoe surface which makes them very durable and long-lasting. This is fine except that this type of brake lining is a bit noisier and more likely to squeal for a long time before it "beds in." The metal surface will also wear out your drums and rotors quicker. Unless you do a lot of hard, fast performance driving, my advice is to stick with the standard or regular asbestos variety of brake lining. Though you will not get the mileage out of them that you would the metallics, they are much easier on your drums and rotors. Standard lining also costs less.

**Combi Kits**—As a mechanic I used to call them combi or combination kits. These are the little springs and hold-down hardware needed to assemble and keep the brake pads and shoes in place. Among some of the pieces are the return springs, nails, hold-down springs and spring seats, hold-down retainers, anti-rattle springs and retainer clips. The packages come for either front disc brakes or rear drum brakes. Most of the pieces work on a spring or spring/wedge principle. The packages can cost anywhere from $10.00 to $15.00 per set. These pieces do not wear so much as lose their tensile strength, and that is really the only reason why they should be replaced—if they lose their tautness or spring. In the case of rear drum brakes, combi kits are designed to push the shoes onto the drum when the brake pedal is applied and pull them back away from the drum when the pedal is released. When a mechanic disassembles brakes, using his special brake tools, he can tell instantly, by "feel," if the springs have lost their strength. He can also observe how snugly the shoes fit against the backing plate by pulling on them, testing their resistance. And many times, he will overstretch a spring himself, or lose one during disassembly.

The fact is, combi kits don't have to be replaced as often as the mechanic usually replaces them. These are the little knick-knacks in a shop's inventory that bring in extra cash flow, above and beyond the price of a standard brake job. If you are confronted by a mechanic who wants to sell you this brake hardware for all four wheels, I would ask him to show me at least five or six stretched or mutilated springs out of the dozen or more on the car.

Too often a mechanic will find one weak spring on one wheel then profess that you need to buy the whole kit because it is preferred to have opposing brakes operating in "identical" fashion. Not only that, he can give you a "scare" line and say that it is very important to safety. I know of mechanics who did just this because they received a small commission for each combi kit sold. The fact is, many mechanics have boxes of extra brake springs, retainers, clips, etc. that are in perfect working order just lying around the shop. He wouldn't think of giving you another spring, but instead he wants to sell you the whole she-bang, a complete set.

The fact that your springs are bad, or ever will be, is a little slim. They hold their tensile strength amazingly well. I've seen cars with well over 100,000 miles with the original combi kits intact and working perfectly. But if it so happens that the mechanic can show you a few over-stretched springs that are not performing their function, yes, make the purchase, but not for both rear wheels. Buy one set for the wheel that has the bad springs. These springs actually should be included in an advertised brake special. Look for the phrase "all minor parts included." When you get to the shop, ask if minor parts are defined as springs and clips. If not, then ask for them to be included. These items are often negotiable, because their cost is negligible compared to the price of the brake job.

**Anchor Blocks**—Mechanics refer to anchor blocks as "adjusters" or "stars." They are little cylinder-type devices located at the bottom of the brake shoes. They expand or contract when adjusted with a brake spoon. This is how the rear brakes on your vehicle are adjusted. However, these anchor blocks often become frozen or immobile. Dirt, water and grime can get into the delicate threads and jam this component, thus making it impossible to adjust your rear brakes properly. But this can be easily corrected by cleaning the adjusting nut and bolt. More often than not, it will work perfectly. Do mechanics do this? Some do; some don't. If a mechanic told me that I needed a new anchor block because he couldn't adjust my brakes I would ask him if he cleaned it. All you have to do to clean it is remove the wheel and drum then detach the anchor block by spreading the brake shoes. I've never seen an anchor block that wouldn't come apart for the purpose of cleaning. There is really no need to buy one—they are dealer only parts in most cases anyway and the wait and charge for one could be considerable.

**Backing Plates**—A backing plate is what your rear brake shoes ride against and it can be faulty when worn. It can only become worn by the repeated action of the brake shoes, which will cause a cut or groove in its surface. This happens in much older vehicles and I would be leery if somebody told me that my backing plate was bad, when I was in possession of a nearly new vehicle. Besides, with a standard brake job the backing plate is routinely wiped clean and lubricated in these spots. It had better be. . . it's part of the brake job.

## SERVICE

What exactly is involved in a brake job? That depends on what you've negotiated up to this point. Some shops offer "complete" brake job specials, but often hidden between the included items are additional charges for services that are necessary but not part of the deal. In worst cases, some services are offered and charged as part of a package but not performed. The following is a list of services that should be *included* in a standard brake job. If they aren't, then insist that they should be or find somewhere else that will perform them.

**Bearings & Grease Seals**—A mechanic doesn't necessarily have to pack the front wheel bearings as a complement to a brake job, but it is a service that should be done at the same time.

Most front drum brakes are on the older vehicles. When the drums are removed from the front wheels there is easy access to the inner and outer bearings of each wheel. In fact, they are right there in plain sight. It does not take any time at all to pack these bearings with new grease, but all too often a mechanic will service the brakes and assemble the wheels without so much as smearing grease on the bearings, let alone packing them.

When the rotors are removed for the purpose of turning, the bearings must be removed and set aside until reassembly. Why can't a mechanic make it a stiff rule to pack the wheel bearings when they are conveniently off the wheel? It takes about five minutes to accomplish the task. If the service is included and appears on the advertisement or coupon it is absolutely essential that they do the work prescribed. Wheel bearings are important. They are under heavy load and pressure, must turn constantly and are subject to extreme heat.

How would you know if your wheel bearings have been packed after a brake job? Real easy: remove the hub caps on the front wheels of your vehicle. You will see a small cup-like cover in the middle of the wheel; it is about the size of a small Dixie cup. Pry this cup off using a screwdriver and look inside the hub. This area is where the outer wheel bearing is seated. If a mechanic has packed the bearings you will see evidence of new grease—new grease is sometimes yellowish or a clear dark green. The new grease should be in profuse amounts on the outside of the outer bearing. Little or no grease or grease that is black is an indication that no bearing pack has been done. If you find that this is the case, and the policy of the shop is to pack the bearings with a brake job, or worse yet, you have been charged for a bearing pack, take the car back and insist that they do the work. Then have them initial it on the invoice for your satisfaction.

Grease seals come with calipers and drums. These seals keep the bearing grease contained inside the hub so it doesn't travel up the spindle and splatter all over the new brakes. Some shops supply grease seals with a standard brake job. Others do not and want to charge you extra for them. Find a brake special that includes grease seals in the deal, if at all possible. If not, make mention to the service manager or mechanic to check the seals to determine if they are in good condition. While you're at it have them examine the rear axle seals to make sure they are not leaking. An axle seal that leaks will ruin a perfectly good set of brake pads or shoes. Who pays for the brakes if they miss this inspection and as a result your rear lining gets contaminated? They pay for the shoes but you pay for the labor to install them!

**Turning Drums & Rotors**—If the drums and rotors are deeply scored with ridges deep enough to catch your fingernail, they should be machined smooth. This is referred to as "turning." It is done by securing drums and rotors on a driveshaft where they spin and come in contact with a diamond tipped bit. The machine has two cutting modes: a rough cut (initial cut) and a fine (final cut). It is the mechanic's job to make as many rough cuts as necessary to obtain a clean smooth surface on the drum or rotor. These cuts are usually made in increments of two-thousandths of an inch. A scored drum might take a cut of eight-thousandths of an inch before it is cleaned up. Then an additional fine cut of two-thousandths to finish it.

Generally, any metal cut more than ten-to twelve-thousandths is exceeding allowable tolerances and sometimes they find this out after the many cuts. Therefore it is quite possible that your drum or rotor did mic out within specification, only the mechanic found out later that it required too many cuts to "clean it up." In this case the shop should notify you and get your verbal approval for the additional expense. This happens sometimes and it is really not the mechanic's fault. Some drums and rotors are scored so unevenly that it is difficult to get an accurate measurement on them. If this should happen, you have every right to demand a measurement of your old drums or rotors when you pick up your car.

> ## CAUTION
>
> *Quite often you'll be told that turning rotors and drums is absolutely necessary for all brake jobs. Quite often, it is included in the entire brake price. However, if the rotors and drums are not pitted or scored, it is not absolutely necessary. With heavy brake use, such as in frequent stop 'n' go traffic, the pads and shoes will wear much faster than the rotors or drums. Therefore, it is possible that you'll only have to replace the pads and shoes, and perhaps have the rotors and drums turned every other brake job.*

Although I haven't seen too many drums or rotors gouged, burned, or ruined by a mechanic who didn't know what he was doing on the lathe, the possibility does exist that a drum or rotor will catch sharply on the machine and stop suddenly. This is because the initial cut in the drum has been set too deep—usually. If you are standing in view of the brake lathe and this happens to one of your drums or rotors and you find out later that this drum or rotor is ruined, then this is obviously the cause, the mechanic was at fault. If you are witness to this, and the drum or rotor is ruined, you have cause for litigation.

What happens all too frequently on the brake lathe is the habit of a mechanic to leave out the fine cut entirely. The reason is that the fine cut takes twice as long to accomplish as the rough cut—the cycle time is doubled. A mechanic in a hurry runs through several rough cuts, checks for smoothness, then pulls it off the lathe. This is a heinous shortcut. The fine or smooth cut does a much better job of cutting a true hard profile into the drum or rotor surface. Smoother and cleaner metal is not as porous. A fine cut produces a firmer, and more positive contact between the drum/rotor surface and the brake pad/shoe. It should always be mandatory. Rushed mechanics don't seem to like waiting around near the brake lathe for a drum/rotor that is taking its sweet time on the fine cut mode. For years, they've been getting away with rough cuts alone. Make sure you get a rough and fine cut if your drums and rotors are going to be turned.

**Arcing Shoes**—While we're still at the brake lathe let's talk about arcing or chamfering the rear brake shoes. Rear brake shoes resemble half circles; they have a curved arc. This arc, on new shoes, is supposed to fit precisely into a drum that has just been turned on the lathe. Many times the fit is not precise and thus the shoe must be arced on the brake lathe machine. The section of the machine that handles this chore has a saddle for the shoe to sit in. A handle is used to move this saddle back and forth, pushing the shoe into a rotating abrasive disk. In this manner the shoe is sanded to the exact same arc or fit as the inside curve of the drum. What do you have? You have a perfect and complete fit with little or no error. It means that the inside drum surface is making 100% direct contact with the shoe—total braking power.

Here's the sad part about arcing shoes. I would estimate that as many as 70% of the mechanics do not perform this function at all. Besides taking additional time, besides being a chore that is mandatory, besides the fact that it ensures safe and adequate brakes from the start, the mechanics have told me that "what the hell, the shoes will break in themselves." This statement is typical of a repair sham. I've conducted many experiments by installing brake shoes that were not arced on a vehicle, taken the car for a test ride, returned to the shop and inspected the results. In every case the new shoes were hitting (making stopping contact) on the outer edges of the shoe lining—a total braking surface area of perhaps 40% of its designed 100% potential. The shoe lining must be custom fit to the arc of the drum, especially after the drum's profile has been changed by cutting it on the lathe.

The statement that the shoes will arc themselves is correct in a primitive sort of way. But it might take thousands of miles for the shoes to seat into the profile of the drum, especially if they haven't been mated to the drum via the arcing procedure. Will it take 1,000 miles to seat, or will it take 6,000 miles? That depends upon how bad they were out of fit to begin with. Why should a customer have to endure a loss of 60% braking efficiency for even a short duration? The reasoning that it will soon be over because the shoes will seat in a while or that the customer will never know, just doesn't hold water. I don't care if they are new shoes, if they are not arced and mated precisely to the drum, the braking power will be reduced. If per chance the mechanic has also left his greasy hand prints on the lining of these non-arced shoes, that car is going to be more difficult to stop than if the job had been performed right. Is that any way for new brakes to be installed on a vehicle especially when you're paying a king's ransom for the job? I think not. You might have had more braking power on your shoes before that bad job was performed!

Insist that the chore of arcing the shoes to fit the drum be performed. This chore is not in the category of extra amenities; it is crucial to the effectiveness of your brakes and should be mandatory.

**Bleeding Brakes**—There are two ways to bleed brakes on a vehicle. One is the manual way involving two mechanics: one mechanic under the car who opens the bleeder valves to bleed out fluid, and the other who sits at the wheel and pumps up the brake pedal to force the brake fluid through the lines. This manual type of operation is very primitive and takes a great deal of time and coordination on the part of both mechanics. It is more subject to human error. Two mechanics just can't seem to get into perfect sync all of the time and as a result one yells "pump em up" and the other mechanic doesn't hear him, or some other mis-cue. As a result, air often stays in the lines no matter how hard these two try to get it out, and this leads to a spongy pedal. The two mechanics conceivably can spend more time, which leads to a higher labor charge, repeating the bleeding for each wheel and still end up with a few air bubbles in the system. They also have to constantly refill the master cylinder. What's more, there is no guarantee that they will flush the lines completely and remove all the old brake fluid. Fluid breaks down in viscosity and chemically. What happens when brakes are bled manually is that not all of the old fluid gets flushed out of the system. In a sense, the old brake fluid dilutes and contaminates the new fluid that enters the lines.

The other way to bleed brakes is by using a power bleeder (a pressurized tank containing brake fluid and connection adapters). By placing an adapter over the master cylinder of a car, a mechanic can turn a valve and produce a steady pressure in the brake lines by which he can bleed off the individual wheels at his leisure. If you saw two brake special ads and one said "bleed and adjust brakes" and the other "power bleed and adjust brakes," go for number two. When a system is power bled using the pressurized tank, a constant and steady flow of fluid is delivered which forces all the old fluid and air out of the system. This is precisely want you want—brand new brake fluid in the entire system without air bubbles.

**Road Testing**—Most repair facilities do not road test each and every vehicle to see if the repairs made solved the problem—but they should. I'd want my vehicle driven for a few miles with the new brake job to insure it was braking at its maximum potential, that there was no air in the lines, and that it had a good high and firm brake pedal.

✔ Learn to recognize the symptoms of faulty brakes—low brake pedal, brake noise, spongy pedal, rapid fluid loss in the master cylinder (wet wheels), brake pull, pulsating pedal and brake drag.

✔ It is time to replace your brakes when you have 30% or less lining left. Have the mechanic show you the comparison of your brake shoes or pads versus new ones. Remember, shoes/pads only need be replaced as axle sets, i.e. both front or both rear. Don't be talked into a "mandatory" four-wheel brake job.

✔ Even new brake lining on your vehicle can become contaminated and ruined by leaking fluid from a worn wheel cylinder. Check inside tires for oily wetness.

✔ Your car might have electronic sensors in your brake lining that tell you, via a dash light, when your lining needs replacement. Check your owner's manual to see if you have such a system on your car.

✔ Wheel cylinders and calipers can be rebuilt economically and they do not have to be replaced except past the point of repair. Insist on rebuilding first before purchasing new ones.

✔ If a mechanic tells you that your drums and rotors are bad you should ask him to prove it by checking the specifications in his shop manual and by showing you his measurement on the drum or rotor itself.

✔ Find out if there is a shop policy regarding used drums and rotors if you happen to need those parts and would like to obtain them for yourself. Ask if they allow you to locate these parts and if they would agree to install them on your vehicle as part of the brake job.

✔ Brake service is one of the most lucrative tickets in a

bonus shop. Monitor the operation very carefully and ask questions about anything that seems confusing or misleading.

✔ When checking a brake special ad pay attention to the services offered such as: rebuilding wheel cylinders, road testing, grease seals, bearing packs, power bleeding and warranty/guarantee.

✔ Drums and rotors should receive a fine (final) cut on a brake lathe. Make sure the shop performs this service—they often don't.

✔ Make certain that your new brake shoes are arced. Arcing insures 100% shoe/drum contact. This service is often skipped by hurried mechanics.

✔ If the mechanics are pushing the combi kits (hold down hardware) on you, there must be a reason. Are all of the springs bad? One bad spring? Does he have an extra? Combi kits are often a negotiable item.

✔ Make sure that your brake shop offers the power bleed service, and that they carry the highest quality brake fluid.

✔ Most anchor blocks are easily serviceable. Request that the shop disassemble and clean these parts before you're talked into purchasing new ones.

✔ For those who do their own brake jobs, be aware that dismantling and pick-a-part yards sell used drums and rotors. Many auto parts stores turn used drums and rotors for you.

✔ Know the difference between metallic (long life) brake lining and standard. Standard asbestos lining is sufficient for any vehicle.

✔ Ask for your old brake parts. If you don't get your old parts, sometimes a lawyer cannot help you with litigation if they don't have some physical evidence. It pays to be prepared.

✔ Ask for a warranty or guarantee in writing. They should come with every brake job and some are better than others. Note whether the shop provides free follow-up service on your new brakes, such as checking and adjusting them at regular mileage intervals.

# 7

# THE FRONT END

## A MAZE OF MANIACAL MECHANICCA

The term "front end" is interpreted by a body repair shop as the area of the car consisting of headlights, grilles and bumpers. But to a mechanic, the front end means the steering and suspension parts underneath the front part of the vehicle. They are those parts that look like pipes, rods, linkages and knotted little metal joints that are mysteriously responsible for holding your wheels together and helping you steer your car down the road. When a mechanic says, "hmmm...she needs some front end work" you are immediately impressed because you know little or nothing about front end parts and their function other than they are somehow important and related to safety. And that's about all most customers know, that this jumble of jack straws under his/her car is essential and important, but the pieces and their exact function are vague—shrouded in mystery. Most auto repair customers know less about front end operation than any other area of auto repair except for maybe electrical. And believe me, I've seen more than one mechanic take advantage of this fact.

# FRONT END COMPONENTS

## U & CV JOINTS

U-joints are couplers at the front and rear of your driveshaft (the long tube that runs underneath your car). In front-wheel-drive cars they are known as CV, or *constant velocity*, joints and they are located in the front end.

Both U-joints and CV joints can cause a severe chassis vibration at certain speeds when they are worn. The whole car will shudder and vibrate considerably when a U-joint begins to go. Perhaps your car runs smoothly up to 35 mph, but at 40 mph everything begins to shake. Maybe at 50 mph the shaking stops and the car smooths out again. These are symptoms of bad or worn U-joints. Also, worn CV joints may produce abnormal effects in steering and handling and a metallic swishing noise.

## WHEEL & AXLE BEARINGS

You could easily pick up the sound of a worn front wheel bearing, or a worn rear axle bearing, by driving slowly near a concrete wall of a building and listening carefully. Generally, a worn wheel or axle bearing will emit a metallic rumbling sound. The noise will be more low pitched than a brake swish, but could present itself when the brakes are applied. Fortunately a mechanic has just to pull the suspect wheel to determine which problem exists, if both are not prevalent. Wheel bearings come in "inner and outer," two for each front wheel. If one bearing fails it is common to replace both bearings on that wheel. However, it is not necessary to replace all four front wheel bearings for both front wheels unless there is bearing failure on both sides.

## BALL JOINTS

Most cars have an upper and lower ball arrangement designed into the front suspension of the vehicle. Each car has one upper and one lower ball joint per side, or four altogether. The lower ball joint is pressed into and rests in the lower control arm, the upper ball joint, in the upper control arm. Both control arms are hinged, to allow the vertical movement of the wheel. The ball joints are ball and socket joints that support a great deal of vehicle weight. Think of the upper ball joint as keeping things steady (the wheel tight) while the lower ball joint does the same but also supports much more of the vehicle's weight.

**Wear**—The lower ball joint often wears out first because it bears more load and receives more direct friction. The upper ball joint frequently lasts the life of the vehicle because it is subjected to less. Routinely, mechanics check the lower ball joint first knowing that it is the better candidate for wear and this is why lower ball joints are replaced frequently. The lower ball joint is equipped with a grease fitting for lubrication (part of the L.O.F.) since it requires constant lubrication to move freely.

Some ball joints are designed with no grease fittings, meaning they are pre-lubed and "factory sealed." Once they are worn they must be replaced. This forces you to buy a part that was non-serviceable to begin with. Many foreign cars have these types of ball joints.

A combination of age and constant movement can cause a ball joint to wear, leading to sloppy or excess movement. If the protective rubber boot is torn or weathered, it can allow sand and grit to cause friction (which causes wear), leading to eventual replacement. Erratic driving habits like jumping curbs, hitting parking stops, accelerating up driveways and rough off-road dirt driving can also wear out a ball joint quickly.

New factory ball joints are riveted or welded to the control arm after they have been pressed into the seat. If they are riveted in, a mechanic has to use an air chisel to remove the rivets so the joint can be pressed out. So in many instances, a mechanic who sees a riveted ball joint knows that it has not been replaced before. Mechanics always bolt on a replacement lower ball joint—they do not rivet or weld new ones back into the control arm. The bolts versus the rivet's situation is something that your mechanic will spot immediately and perhaps it is one thing that you should also know about your car. When checking out a used, near-new car, check to see if the lower ball joints have been replaced by noting if they have been bolted on.

**Diagnosing**—What does a mechanic do to determine if the lower ball joints are bad and likely to cause problems with alignment and tire wear? The diagnosis is subject to some backyard tricks and speculations on the part of the mechanic. The relative condition of the ball joints can be gauged but not as precisely as many other vehicle parts. A few years ago, most shops relied on a *Lomac*, a large diagnostic tool shaped like a huge "C" with a dial gauge. It was a highly inaccurate tool that cinched the upper and lower control arms to detect any movement in the ball joints. A mechanic had only to summon the customer over and show him this impressive dial reading to convince him that he had excessive play in the front end ball joints. Excessive play meant that the ball joints were bad and had to be replaced. You would be surprised how many customers did not question the authenticity of this Lomac tool, but instead signed quickly for the repair work. I personally witnessed hundreds of ball joints sold via this scenario. Today the Lomac has been banned by law and is not or should not be used as a legitimate and accurate piece of diagnostic equipment. If you ever see a mechanic using this device, or something similar to it, disclaim the faulty diagnosis and take your vehicle to another repair facility.

Another way to determine if a lower ball joint is bad is to wiggle the grease fitting underneath it. The grease fitting, if it has one, is attached directly to the bottom of the ball under the control arm. If the grease fitting moves it means that the ball is "floating" in the socket, indicating a worn joint. This is excluding the fact that the grease fitting itself is loose. This procedure has to be done under a load; that is, the car should not be up on the rack to make this test. Ironically, this simple procedure is indicated as standard diagnosis in most of the large repair manuals.

I have already discussed how a torn ball joint boot can convince a mechanic that the lower ball joint has come to some harm as a result of contamination. The only problem is that the mechanic doesn't really know how long that boot has been damaged and how long that ball joint has been subjected to debris. Even if the ball joint appears good (tight) he would most likely suggest that you repair it at once and replace the unit. Boots do not come in separate packages—they are part of the ball joint kit. They will suggest that you replace both lower ball joints (both sides of the vehicle).

What if one ball joint checks out bad and the other appears to be perfect? Well, you could argue the case, especially on a newer vehicle with low mileage and convince him that right now you don't want two and that he should install one. His defense will be "Well, the other is sure to follow since it's received the same amount of wear." I've heard the same thinking when it involves front wheel bearings; "When one side goes the other is sure to follow." Is this law? Is this true? Not really, but it sure sounds good, doesn't it? The mechanics of today have had it so good with the "replace everything in sets" syndrome that when it comes down to fixing only what is broken, they resist at every turn.

It is safe to say that replacing ball joints is a once-in-a-vehicle lifetime necessity. It's doubtful that your car will have to undergo this type of repair more than once, or even once, but if it should, the rule of "second opinions" is the advised way to go. Virtually anybody could tell you that the ball joints were bad, even a tire buster, but I would advise you to seek out a mechanic wearing the front end patch or the alignment mechanic.

**Other Considerations**—A worn ball joint will affect toe-in and camber because it affects the relative position of the tire. Too much play in the lower ball joint lets the tire recover sloppily from a minor jolt or a sudden turn. This puts your front end temporarily out of alignment and this, in itself, wears tires. After you have lower ball joint repair on your car you will be told that an alignment is necessary to put the front end back to specifications. The alignment recommendation is certainly justified even as a precautionary measure (many shops throw in an alignment for free with such front-end work).

If your car was diagnosed as having bad lower ball joints and you were urged to replace all four (upper and lowers), I would not follow this advice for reasons stated previously. Ball joints do not need to be replaced in sets.

## TIE ROD ENDS

Tie rod ends function like ball joints, but they have a ball and sleeve design, are smaller and they help steer the car instead of supporting its weight. The tie rods are actually the bars that connect the bottom of the steering shaft with the spindles that are attached to the wheels. The longest leverage bar is called the *drag* or *center link*. Attached to the center link are the tie rod bars that turn the wheels. Tie rod ends are subject to push and pull stress as a result of the forces applied during vehicle steering and cornering. They wear in the same fashion as ball joints and must be lubricated frequently. At the bottom of the tie rod end is a grease fitting (some have none and are factory sealed) for lubing.

**Diagnosing**—The most common way for a mechanic to check the condition of a tie rod end is with the use of a pair of *channel locks*. While the car is racked, he compresses the tie rod end with the channel locks and watches for movement in the tire. A second mechanic is often required to watch the tire while he performs this simple test. Movement in the wheel indicates excessive play in the tie rod end joint. In this manner, tie rod ends are easier to diagnose since they are smaller, isolated and not part of another system. Like the ball joint, when a tie rod end has a loose grease fitting this points to a worn ball and sleeve and it is therefore time to replace it. Such worn tie rod ends will affect alignment, specifically toe-in and also promote abnormal tire wear.

Worn tie rods may be first noticed in the steering wheel as a lump, bump or grind when making a tight turn or as a grinding/thumping noise while turning the wheel at a dead stop. The steering wheel could feel like it was "knotting" up or binding. If it does, even slightly, this is cause for concern. A worn steering box worm gear would also produce symptoms similar to these, and might even produce too much "free play" in the steering wheel. Either condition is cause for immediate concern and attention. If an outer tie rod end snapped, the wheel in this case would not have any directional support. It would be a case of your wheel going bowlegged or knock-kneed instantly and without warning.

## THE IDLER ARM

The idler arm is an L-shaped rod in the front end that is usually attached to the car's frame and joins the drag, or center link. Its purpose is two-fold; it supports the tie rod bars and drag link, and allows them to turn smoothly without binding. Since the drag link and tie rod bars are very heavy, the repeated shocks and bumps associated with normal driving could damage or bend these parts. It is the job of the idler arm to absorb the heavy shock and vibrations of these long linkage parts and at the same time provide steady support that allows the linkages to turn and recover smoothly.

Most idler arms have a rubber bushing sandwiched between two large flat washers. It is this rubber bushing that absorbs the repeated pounding and shocks when you take a bad dip at high speed, drive too fast over a speed bump or clip a curb. After a while, the bushing simply compresses, wears out, or becomes weathered due to road debris, water and grit. Many idler arms have two joints similar in function to tie rod ends: one joint connects to the drag link, and the other is a swivel joint that connects the idler arm to the frame or body of the car. Many times idler arms are equipped with grease fittings at both swivel joints; then again, many are factory sealed and replaced when they are worn. Generally speaking, you can consider the idler arm a crude shock absorber for the front end parts.

**Diagnosis**—A mechanic often determines if the idler arm is bad with a simple test to determine excess play in the part. With both wheels suspended above the ground, either by a jack under the frame or crossmember, or with the car on a shop rack, he visually locates the idler arm then he pushes the tire in and out, keeping an eye on the idler arm and how far it moves. If the idler arm is noticeably worn it will jump vertically up and down while he is doing this pull/push test. More than a half-inch of movement would be cause for concern. Again, the make of the automobile and the tolerance allowed by the manufacturer's specification book will be the final determining factor. Make sure you see the mechanic with the car up in the air. There is no other way for him to diagnose the problem. If he tells you the movement is beyond the tolerance set by the manufacturer, ask to see where it is so written and for a demonstration of the excess play.

It is safe to assume if the idler arm moves more than an inch it is definitely becoming worn—the bushing has lost its flexibility and resiliency. Keep in mind that many idler arms have grease fittings and they should be lubricated as part of the L.O.F. (lube, oil and filter). If a new idler arm is installed on your vehicle just make sure the mechanic lubricates it if it has the fittings for such. A factory sealed idler arm cannot be lubed and is simply replaced when it is worn.

## CONTROL ARM BUSHINGS

Upper and lower control arm bushings are made of rubber and similar in design to the idler arm bushing. They are located on the inside of the fender well, behind the wheel. There is typically one lower control arm bushing in the lower control arm and it is larger, again depending upon the make of the vehicle. Two bushings are located in the upper control arm, which in this case makes for three bushings per side. We will talk about the diagnosis and replacement of the upper control arm bushings that are generally found on General Motors products; this would be the two upper bushings per side, or the four of them altogether.

**What They Do**—The upper control arms and bushings allow for the vertical (up-and-down) movement of the front end chassis. They work much like a hinge or lever and the bushings themselves absorb shock so as to delete the transmission of hard jars and bumps to the frame of the car. They suffer twisting and torque pressures and are subjected to moderate amounts of weight load.

The bar connecting both ends of the upper control arm is surrounded and encased by the bushings. These bushings can become worn by repeated movement or they can become weathered and rotted. Sometimes the rubber bushing fabric can be seen splitting away from the bushing sleeve and projecting out from the control arm, which is a clear indication that the rubber bushing is deteriorating. Upper control arm bushings commonly have grease fittings at their outermost ends and are lubricated in the same way as the other front end parts.

**Diagnosing**—Diagnosing upper control arm bushings can present some problems for the novice mechanic. In my younger days as a department store R & R mechanic, I was convinced there was only one way to solve a problem—MINE. Such was the way I felt when I was confronted one day with a customer who came into our shop with a loud squeaking problem.

He had a newer model Chevrolet and when I pushed the front of his hood up and down and listened to this familiar sound, I was positively convinced that I knew what was causing it. Nine times out of ten, as it had been with me, this annoying rusty hinge clamoring noise had pointed to bad upper control arm bushings. The bushings had always been torn, dry and squeaking: the solution was to replace them and the noise would go away. It had usually worked before, and I was quite cocky in my sales pitch to this customer. Only he became quite suspicious and frugal-minded when I told him that the repair package would include replacing both sets at considerable expense. I was, after all, operating on commission. He was not so easily taken. First, he had me spray the bushings with W-D 40 to his satisfaction, to rule out the possibility that they could be externally lubricated. Next, he made me use my stethoscope on the part to isolate the problem area and make sure that it was the bushings at fault. After several more precautionary maneuvers on my part to convince him that I did indeed know what I was talking about, (and that he didn't) I had him sign the work order for the prescribed repair. He did so very reluctantly.

It took me about about two hours to complete the work, whereupon I lowered the car to the ground and immediately heard that wretched squeaking hinge noise! I shoved down hard on the front end of the vehicle but the noise was as prominent as ever. Uh-oh. I spent the next hour climbing around that Chevy hunting down the elusive squeak. Meanwhile the customer called, irritated that it was taking too long; he needed his car. Panic set in. I already knew that I had misdiagnosed this vehicle and charged the customer with major front end work that he obviously did not need. Worse yet, I hadn't found the real problem for the loud squeak, and if I didn't find it I would be caught red-handed, with an irate customer on my hands holding a whopping repair receipt. Lastly, I was tying up a rack and the rest of my scheduled workload was choking the parking lot. As a last resort, I examined the upper ball joint then looked at the rest of the grease fittings on the other front end parts. Instantly I noticed that this car had been lubricated some time ago but when I looked at the upper ball joint, it did not show signs of lubrication—the previous mechanic had missed it, or had forgotten about it. The instant I lubricated the upper ball joint the noise went away. Naturally, I lubed the rest of the front end parts thinking desperately that this act was some kind of penance on my part. Thoughts of inspectors from the Bureau and lawsuits flashed through my mind.

A minute later the Chevy owner showed up demanding his old/new bushing parts. He paid his bill in a huff, and screeched off the parking lot. I saw him one hour later. The customer then began to berate me with the news that he had his old bushings checked out by another mechanic and was told that they were in perfect shape, or appeared to be, before they had been so ruthlessly torn out of his vehicle. He demanded satisfaction. In no way did I think about telling this man that I had made a mistake—I was committed. Nor was I about to mention to him that I had forgotten about performing an alignment (which he had been charged for) because I was so pressed for time. All the shop's mechanics came to my aid, and together we stood our ground and argued as to why the bushings needed to be replaced. Moments later the guy left, much to my relief.

How will a mechanic check out the condition of your upper control arm bushings? Well, not entirely as in the previous example. Although squeaks and torn bushing material can assist in the determination, there is a better way, one that is used often. It involves using two mechanics, one on the ground, the other up in the racked car's driver seat. While one mechanic applies the brake pedal, the other mechanic below tries to forcibly turn the front wheel in either direction. A firm wrenching motion back and forth works best. If the upper joints have any excess play in them, or if the bushing is compressed or worn, it will show up in the excessive movement of the tire. This testing procedure isolates the control arm bushing and determines its fit or relative tightness. Bad or worn upper control arm bushings can have a direct effect on the wheel alignment of your vehicle. Such worn parts can throw off all the measurements.

It is strongly advised that your car be aligned properly after such work. Many control arms have shims that are used in the alignment procedure. Sometimes a mechanic can mistakenly lose a shim or two while he is removing the control arms from the vehicle, in which case he will have to replace them with new ones once he aligns the car. It bears repeating that the front end man should be doing the front end work unless the other shop mechanics are equally trained in this area.

## SHOCKS

The shock absorber is really a simple part in function and concept. It consists of an oil-filled tube that contains a rod and piston, and some high pressure seals. The rod that extends out of the top of the shock connects to the car chassis, in many cases up under the fender well. The bottom part of the shock absorber connects near or on the lower control arm or other similar suspension part. It is the job of the shock absorber, in conjunction with the leaf or coil spring, to dampen and nearly eliminate the shock and vibration transmitted to the car frame or chassis via the tire-to-road contact. It does this by the action of the piston in the fluid-filled tube when force is applied upon the shock bar or shaft. The fluid in the shock is kept within a sealed and pressurized environment. The piston travels up and down in the tube with high resistance from the fluid. Thus the shaft moves against this resistance slowly in either direction. You can liken the action of a shock absorber to a pencil stuck in a clump of hard tar. Pulling the pencil out of the tar is just as difficult as pushing it in— equal force in both directions.

In addition to absorbing road shock and vibration, the shock also serves to keep its respective tire flat to the pavement at all times. This is important while driving over hilly terrain, speed bumps, dips, curbs, pot holes and other obstacles.

**Wear**—Shocks wear out when the piston wears in the bore of the tube, or when a seal breaks and it loses its fluid. It simply loses its capacity to create resistance and the ride becomes noticeably rougher. According to the repair manuals I have read, the general consensus is that you should replace your original (new factory shocks) at about the 50,000 mile mark; they give no reason for this other than it is non-specific practical advice. Mechanics also drool when they examine a car with factory-equipped shocks. Many believe that the original man-ufacturer's shock absorber is somehow substandard and prone to pre-mature failure. This thinking is prevalent throughout the repair in-dustry with the exception of the dealership mechanic and his obvious debate.

**Replacement**—Just when should you replace your shocks? It de-pends. For instance, a person who car pools with three or four in-dividuals in city traffic (suffering the bumps and grinds of gridlock), and does this day after day for years, has not subjected his car to the same wearing forces that an older person would driving moderate speeds in the country with no passengers. Someone who tows a boat or trailer behind him on a fairly regular basis and drives mountain switchbacks and dirt roads is going to replace his shocks faster than one who makes infrequent trips. A four-wheel drive truck or dirt vehicle is certainly going to impose more stress on the suspension of a vehicle than one who rarely drives off the shoulder. There are people in this world who will drive the same way to work every day, forever hitting that frightfully deep rain gutter every morning every time and at the same speed. There are drivers who drive very hard over speed bumps and curbs, bottoming out their suspension parts to where metal meets metal. And there are the others who truly believe that their car is an animate object, treating it as delicately as a cherished pet. So just who says that you "gotta replace them there shocks every 50,000 miles?" If you want to, go ahead, but try a few things first to see if they really need it.

**Diagnosing**—First, look under your car and locate your shock absorbers. Look for fluid leakage which will darken the lower half of the shock, or appear grime-covered. There might even be some black sand adhering to the bottom of the shock. If you see this it means that a seal is blown in the shock and has leaked fluid. A leaking shock should be replaced.

If one shock on one side needs to be replaced, so does the other side, but not necessarily the other end. In other words, if the right rear shock needs to be replaced, so does the left rear, but if the fronts are okay, then they don't have to be. Opposing suspension parts must be kept equal in strength and condition. Obviously, if your car leans abnormally to one side, right or left, or dips in one corner, the condition of the shock would be suspect. If at all possible, grasp each shock and wiggle it to make sure that it has not broken away from its mount. It should be immovable and firm to the hand hold. If you can see the tops of your front shocks with your hood open wiggle the top of the threaded shaft, making sure that it is tight. Inspect the rubber grommets at this point and make sure that the retaining nut is tight.

If your shocks pass all these tests, you can perform a *rebound test*. Two people work best for this procedure. You will need one individual to step on the front bumper of your car. With his hands on the hood for balance, this person should begin to bounce up and down on the vehicle several times then step backwards off the bumper. The rocking motion of the car will continue and the observing person should note how many times the car bounces on its own weight and momentum. A rule of thumb says that a car with good shocks should not bounce any more than two-and- a-half times before it comes to a dead rest. If the car heaves once then stills, certainly it has good shocks. This procedure works well on the rear of the vehicle, too. A safer and more recommended way to do this rebound test is by pushing down hard with the hands on the bumper or hood to start this rocking motion.

**Types Of Shocks**—Almost every shop advertises "heavy-duty" shocks. Heavy-duty simply means that the shock that they are going to sell you is physically larger, has a larger cylinder bore and piston and it will last a bit longer than the original manufacturer's shock absorber. Generally, if you carry along a lot of weight and drive frequently over rough roads, heavy-duty shocks are a good bet.

*Adjustable ride shocks* are shocks that have a turning notch system incorporated into the tube assembly. Before the shock is installed a mechanic can make a physical adjustment on the shock by setting it into a position that denotes a specific characteristic. Three settings are usually possible, including: soft, moderate or regular, or firm—or words to that effect. The soft setting would be a more comfortable ride for someone who does not load the vehicle down heavily. The normal position would be used for normal or ordinary vehicle use in which the driver would drive at the speed limit and perhaps load the car or carry passengers on occasion. The firm setting would be used for heavy loads with more passengers and perhaps extended off-road trips, towing utility vehicles, or high performance driving.

I shouldn't have to tell you that the normal or regular position is where most people have their setting. And this works out to be about the equivalent performance that a heavy-duty shock has. It's ironic; people pay more for these adjustable shocks and end up aborting their potential. It really doesn't hurt to put this kind of shock on the firm or very firm setting. This position comes in handy for heavy loads and the ride is not that much more uncomfortable.

*Air shocks* are commonly installed on the rear of the vehicle only. They are specifically designed to accommodate very heavy loads and towing packages. By the use of a standard tire valve, air shocks can be softened, or stiffened for virtually any load consideration. The plus comes when you realize that by adding air to these shocks you can find any desired ride comfort that suits you. You can also adjust the rear height of your vehicle up or down as much as six to eight inches either way. If you are towing a trailer with a very heavy tongue weight with a back seat full of kids and suitcases, you will soon appreciate how effective air shocks can be. A few squirts of an air hose and up goes the curb height of your vehicle, not to mention these shock's capacity to take the burdensome load off your other suspension parts. If perchance one of the plastic air lines is severed, and the air escapes, the shocks will still function as normally as a heavy-duty shock. If you're willing to part with a few extra dollars, this is the place to do it.

## MACPHERSON STRUTS

I have fewer kind words for the MacPherson strut, which has become the norm in the front end suspension design of most of today's newer cars, especially those with front-wheel-drive. I'm thoroughly convinced that the MacPherson shock was designed to filch money from the repair customer and kill mechanics on the workbench. It is complicated, expensive and difficult to work on. I have seen many coupon specials for both regular heavy-duty shocks and MacPherson struts. A regular two-shock special for $24.95 is a great bargain in anyone's book. A coupon special for two MacPherson shocks at $99.99 (installed) is supposed to be a great bargain also. The difference is a result of the high labor costs required to install the MacPherson variety. In addition, as in the example of the Dodge Rampage and Plymouth Scamp, if the mechanic does not mark the cam location while removing the strut assembly, the vehicle will surely have to be realigned at additional expense. (On these makes the strut bolts to the steering knuckle).

**Diagnosing**—Faulty or worn MacPherson struts are generally diagnosed with the rebound test, much in the same manner as regular shocks.

**Replacement**—The main difference between a regular shock and the MacPherson type is that the regular shock is usually mounted independent of the coil spring. The MacPherson shock has a cartridge loaded into a strut damper assembly that is seated between an upper mounted assembly and a lower knuckle. The coil-spring surrounds the strut damper assembly and is also sandwiched between the upper mount assembly and the lower knuckle. At the top of the MacPherson shock is a rebound stop that holds the shock in place. There is not much point in explaining the rest of the parts; there are many, to be sure. Suffice it to say, the removal of the strut damper assembly is quite involved, including the bench work that must be performed to install the replacement cartridge. It should be stated that the cartridge only is replaced and not the damper assembly, coil spring, or other connecting hardware, so don't let a mechanic sell you these items unless they are obviously defective.

## SCARE TACTICS

I had a lady friend call me up in desperation one day. She explained to me over the phone that her foreign car dealership had found a very serious problem with her "whatchamacallit. . . see-see joint. No, boot seal? No, it was the see-boot joint. . . what the heck, they said that my wheel was going to fall off!" I deduced that she meant a "CV joint", or constant velocity joint on a car with front-wheel-drive.

The point to this is that a dishonest mechanic will use three common scare tactics to sell you front end parts. You've just read the all time number one draft choice: "If you don't get this front end part your wheel might fall off." The second most common phrase will be something like: "This part affects your steering drastically." The last one is very effective since the alignment mechanic has penned it as his most favorite expression: "Can't align your car with a bad front end part like this. . . oh, no. You'll have to get it replaced before the alignment." Just remember you will hear losing a wheel, losing your steering, or not able to align, as the most frequent and persistent reasons for front end work. Another stock phrase used in addition to the others is, "If you don't fix that front end part you'll wear those new expensive tires to pieces."

Just how valid are all these claims? Well, the tire wear problem probably holds more water than any of the others put together. Because when we are talking about wheels falling off, and losing your steering, we aren't talking about a problem so bad that it has gone undetected almost forever. In the case of my lady friend, I resented deeply, became irate, over the fact that some high pressure shop had the audacity to scare her like they did, nearly frightening her witless! She had driven her car home at a crawl, and parked it with the intention of never driving it again until she could remedy this mysterious CV joint problem (which turned out to be a split rubber boot that surrounded the CV joint—not the joint itself. Nevertheless she was sold the CV joint as well). This problem wrestled with my conscience because she had a new car. What I objected to was the manner of extreme urgency in which they made the sale—very quickly. Life threatening. A very ugly form of "boo" tactic.

✔ Beware of scare tactics when going in for front end work. If the problem is major get a second or third opinion.

✔ Remember that lower ball joints might wear out once in the lifetime of a car. You will not need two or three sets.

✔ Shop for the best deal for front end parts. Specials or package deals for lower ball joints and upper control arm bushings are frequently announced in many newspapers. It beats paying the per hour labor charge of other repair facilities. A front end alignment is generally included, or should be. Shop around to find a place that offers it as part of the package.

✔ Regular lubrication is the best prevention against premature front end part failure. Be sure that with each L.O.F all zerk fittings have been greased.

✔ Sloppy or excessive steering play, bumping and grinding in the front end area, are signals that a front end part might be worn and in need of replacement.

✔ Abnormal tire wear such as cups, scalloped edges and feathering, can indicate that the front end is misaligned or that new front end parts are needed.

✔ Erratic driving habits like jumping curbs, hitting parking stops hard, accelerating up driveways and rough off-road dirt driving can wear out all front end parts prematurely.

✔ Beware of the Lomac type tool for diagnosing lower ball joints. Such tools are not legal for use any longer. If a mechanic is going to inspect the ball joints, ask what tools he uses. If he says a Lomac, go somewhere else.

✔ Replacing upper and lower ball joints at the same time is unusual. Lower ball joints are more frequently replaced, and uppers last much longer.

✔ All front end parts should be diagnosed by the certified front end mechanic or the alignment mechanic.

✔ Remember that it is common practice to align a car after it has had front end work. The wheels must be reset to manufacturer's specifications. Make sure this is specified on the repair order before you sign for it.

✔ Tie rod ends help steer your car. Therefore, they are the most crucial front end part when dealing with safety. Have them routinely checked if you are having any other front end work done.

✔ For the precise diagnosis of worn front end parts, sophisticated dial-indicator gauges should be used. Ask that these specialty tools be used when your front end parts are inspected.

✔ Loud squeaks do not mean that the upper control arm bushings are bad. Have upper control arm bushings double-checked by the mechanic, making certain they are defective before replacing them.

✔ Perform the push and rebound test to determine the condition of your shock absorbers. Also check for leaks on the shock shaft body. Shocks that rebound more than 2-1/2 times, or leak, need replacement.

✔ Air shocks are a good investment when towing heavy packages over an extended period of time.

✔ Search out the best deals on MacPherson struts. They can be very expensive, especially on some of the foreign vehicles. Advertised specials are run on MacPherson shocks in many newspapers and trade publications.

# 8

# ELECTRICAL SYSTEM

## A CASE OF BAD NERVES

The electrical system in your car can be likened to the central nervous system in your body. Without it, none of the other organs can function. Generally, electrical system malfunctions are extremely difficult to locate, because there are, quite simply, so many things that can go wrong. The problem could be anything from a blown fuse to a defective starter.

When you turn your key to the "Start" position, a myriad of things happen instantly. Electricity is supplied by the battery, routing it to the electronic engine control computer (if your car is so equipped) which goes to a "start" mode to activate the fuel pump to supply extra fuel for starting. Simultaneously the starter receives its charge and spins the flywheel, which is connected to the crankshaft in your engine between the rear of the engine and the transmission. The crankshaft rotates the pistons which build compression in the cylinders. The coil also receives electricity and sends it to the distributor, which routes it to the spark plugs that ignite the compressed air/fuel mixture in your cylinders, and PRESTO! the car starts and you're off to the grocery store. In a perfect world, this happens every time you start your car.

Now I could write an entire book on the electrical system of your car, as many people have. There are numerous books on the subject if you care to know more. But for our purposes, I'll limit the discussion to batteries, starters and alternators (the starting and charging circuits). These parts can certainly be considered R & R components. They are frequently diagnosed, removed and replaced as a regular staple in auto repair. My purpose is to inform you how these systems interact with each other, how they should be maintained and what you can expect when these parts need to be replaced.

## BATTERIES

The battery's main function is to supply initial voltage boost to start the engine. Thereafter, it supplies voltage to sub-systems that require it. It is continually recharged by the alternator, which supplies electricity to the battery when the engine is running. To know why batteries malfunction a little theory on their operation is necessary.

## FUNCTION
The battery performs the following four basic functions in a vehicle:

1. It supplies a surge of electrical energy to the starter motor for the purpose of starting the engine and to the ignition system while the engine is being started.
2. It supplies electricity for the accessories such as the radio, tape deck, heater and lights when the engine is not running and the ignition switch is in the "OFF" or the "Accessory" position.
3. It supplies additional electricity for the accessories while the engine is running when the output of the alternator is exceeded by the various extra accessories. If the output of the alternator is abnormally low the battery will supply the needed energy to operate the component or accessory.
4. The battery stabilizes voltage in the electrical system. Maximum operation of the ignition system and any other electrically operated device is hampered by a damaged, shorted, weak or even an undercharged battery. Many accessories operating at once demands that a battery be in peak condition to supply the demand of all components.

## MAINTENANCE FREE
Not too long ago, batteries came with filler caps and needed to be periodically checked to make sure the distilled water level was high enough to sustain a proper electrolyte level. Today the *sealed battery*, or what is referred to as "maintenance free" or "freedom" battery, is much

more common. Sealed batteries have a different chemistry and construction which provides some advantages over the older model. For one thing, sealed batteries do not have to be checked and adjusted for low battery water. The battery is completely sealed except for two small vent holes on the side. These vent holes allow minute amounts of gas to escape, a necessary breathing device. But the special chemistry composition inside the battery reduces the production of gas to such an extremely small amount that it is nearly undetectable at normal charging voltages.

The sealed battery is almost impervious to the damaging effects of overcharge. The terminals are tightly sealed to minimize leakage, and on many models you can find a charge indicator, or an electronic eye that shows the battery's present state of charge. As an added bonus, compared to an older make or conventional battery in which performance decreases steadily with age, the sealed battery delivers more available power at any time during its life. The sealed battery has a reduced tendency to self-discharge as compared to the older conventional battery.

## DIAGNOSING

There are many reasons why a battery can discharge or appear to be defective. It is all too easy to just blame the battery and have it replaced. As a preliminary test, turn on your headlights. Normally, a discharged battery can be seen in the relative brightness of the headlights. Dim headlights likely indicate a weak or partially discharged battery.

However, there are many other factors that could be responsible for the symptoms of a dead battery. Your mechanic should know these

---

### CAUTION

*Damage to a battery occurs frequently when a car stalls and panicked owners keep desperately turning the key to start the engine. Trying to start a vehicle for overly long periods (over 30 seconds) causes extreme amperage draw and, in some cases, can damage the battery cables and melt their protective insulation. It can also warp and damage the positive and negative plates. Such persistent starting can also damage the windings of the starter motor. It is best to attempt starting in short intervals to allow the electrical circuits to cool somewhat and recover before trying to restart. A hard-starting engine should not be confused with a bad battery or starter, particularly if the cranking speed of the starter is fast and the battery energy is at maximum. A poorly tuned engine can also be the cause.*

symptoms as should you. Don't be talked into purchasing a battery on the spot. The following are some of the common conditions that could discharge a good battery:

1. Leaving the headlights in the "ON" position or the car doors ajar, which would leave the dome light on, would discharge the battery over a short period of time. Leaving a tape deck or radio on, that was hooked directly to a positive lead instead of the fuse block, would also drain the battery.
2. The continued and excessive use of vehicle accessories with the engine not running could cause a direct drain on the battery. The more accessories used, the larger the energy draw.
3. A broken or worn alternator belt. This condition would prevent the alternator from recharging the battery when the engine is running.
4. The improper installation of aftermarket accessories: fog lights, stereos, etc. They may have been wired to a circuit to a point where it overloads and shorts out, producing excessive drain.
5. A battery that has corroded inner plates or a battery case that has been physically damaged allowing battery acid to escape.
6. Loose or corroded battery terminal connections or damaged battery cables. Extremely long battery cables can, over an extended period, put an additional load on the battery and build up resistance.
7. Low alternator output or unusually low RPM's at engine idle.
8. High resistance in the charging circuit caused by other loose electrical connections.
9. A defective starter that draws more amperage than normal.
10. A battery that has been sitting for a long period in an unattended vehicle—which could be from several weeks to several months.

**Troubleshooting**—Most repair facilities can test the condition of your battery. The service is usually free of charge, or should be, and while they are at it they often check the charging system to determine if the alternator is at fault. If they don't, request that they do before purchasing a new battery.

With a non-sealed battery a *hydrometer* can be used to measure the specific gravity of the electrolyte in each cell. There are many types of hydrometers available, the least expensive consisting of a glass tube, a rubber bulb at the end of the tube and a floating device within the tube.

Simply sucking up some of the electrolyte from each cell and examining the position of the float can tell you what condition your battery is in. The increments on the tube might be colored sections that denote words such as "no charge," "poor," "fair," "good," and "full charge." Note that the car does not have to be running while a hydrometer check is being made.

A sealed or maintenance-free battery is commonly *load tested*, with a box-like mechanism that has two leads connected to it, one positive and the other negative. The mechanic hooks up the test leads to the appropriate positive and negative poles on the battery.

He pushes a button which simulates a cranking load (putting the battery under normal strain) and counts down a specific time interval. He releases the button and watches a dial indicator noting how fast the needle is recovering from the load shock and where the needle eventually ends up on the dial: poor, good, full charge, etc. This is a perfect way to simulate a start condition without having to run the engine.

**Charging**—There are two separate methods of recharging batteries which differ in the time or rate of the charge. *Slow charging* is the best and only method of completely charging a battery to its maximum capacity. Slow charging is safe and can be used under almost any condition provided the electrolyte level is sufficient and the condition of the battery is good (good cells). The normal charging rate is about 5 amperes, sometimes a bit more. A fully charged battery is in evidence when all cell specific gravities do not increase when checked at three one-hour intervals and all cells are gassing freely. Charging periods of

## CAUTION

*When batteries are under a charge, highly explosive hydrogen and oxygen gases form in each battery cell. Some of this gas escapes through the vent holes in the plugs on top of the battery case and forms an explosive atmosphere surrounding the battery. This explosive gas lingers in or around the immediate vicinity of the battery, sometimes for hours after the battery has been charged. Sparks or flames can ignite this mixture and cause a dangerous battery explosion, spewing acid everywhere. So don't smoke, or disconnect live circuits. Always shield your eyes when working around batteries, whether they are being charged or not.*

up to 24 hours are not uncommon to completely resaturate a battery but, realistically, from two to six hours is the more common practice.

The other method, known as a *quick charge*, is best for something like a roadside emergency, or to charge the battery for a load test. With a quick charge (much faster ampere rate) the battery isn't fully charged back up to its maximum, but up to an acceptable level of charge for the purpose of starting the vehicle, whereupon the alternator can take over to get the battery back up to maximum. The quick charge poses problems if it is done with too high a rate. This may warp or mutate the interior battery plates. Quick charging is very hard on a battery and should not be used repeatedly as a remedy to replenish the battery's charge. The possibility of battery explosion with a faulty battery under quick charge is a grim reality.

A fast charge takes anywhere from 15 minutes to an hour, and you shouldn't be charged the same fee for both types. The extra time and the additional money spent for a slow charge is the preferred way to go. Don't ever let mechanics fast charge your battery, unless you are in an extreme emergency.

## REPLACEMENT

If your battery needs to be replaced, be sure to choose one with the same capacity and voltage as the one supplied with the car. In some cases higher capacity rated batteries can be installed, depending on the manufacturer's recommendation in your owner's manual. If you don't have an owner's manual, the repair shop should have the information available.

**Undersize**—The use or purchase of an undersized (below rating) battery can result in poor performance and early failure.

For instance, in cold climates the cranking energy needed to start the engine increases with falling temperatures. Sub-zero temperatures can reduce a battery's efficiency to 45% of its potential output and at the same time increase the energy required to turn over the engine by 3-1/2 times over normal weather starting conditions.

On the opposite end, hot weather can also place excessive energy loads on the battery. You'll notice this when you attempt to start your car shortly after a hot engine has been turned off or stalls.

---

### CAUTION

*I don't recommend installing a battery yourself if you do not know the correct procedure. Batteries are very dangerous to work with, especially for the layman who has never installed one, filled it with acid, and charged it. Installation should be free from a facility. However if you must "carry out" a battery and take it home to install in your vehicle, follow the guidelines outlined nearby under Installing It Yourself.*

---

**Oversize**—Buying a battery of higher capacity, quality and rating is wise if you've installed a lot of accessories (mega stereo, telephone, radar detector, alarm, etc.) which all add up to extra load on a standard battery. Campers with extra clearance lights, tow packages that require additional wiring harnesses, high amp and watt stereos and other aftermarket accessories put more demand on a battery than it was originally designed for. Even when very heavy electrical loads are encountered, a higher output alternator that will supply additional charge at low speeds may be required to increase battery life and improve battery performance. The less demand put on a battery at any given time, the better chance the battery has in recovering without harm or permanent damage.

## INSTALLING IT YOURSELF

If you should have to replace the battery in your car yourself, there are a few logical steps—some do's and don'ts. Careless installation of a new battery can ruin it as well as yourself. When removing the old battery, check the position of the positive and negative poles and size up its position in the battery tray with the profile of the new battery.

The replacement battery must be installed in the same position as the old one; sometimes the battery cables will not reach the terminals if the pole positions are reversed.

Always remove the negative ground cable first by using an open end wrench to loosen the clamp (some terminals must be spread by the use of a screwdriver). If the nut is very tight, use one wrench on the head of the bolt and the other on the nut to avoid straining and possibly cracking the top of the cover. Using box-end wrenches works best since they don't have a tendency to strip the nuts.

Special battery pliers are available in stores and can be used on bolts and nuts that have been damaged. A pair of vise grips might be needed to remove a stubborn nut and bolt.

If a battery cable terminal is corroded to the post, do not try to loosen it by hammering or by resting a tool on the battery and prying upwards—either method can break the battery cover or uproot the terminal shaft.

---

## CAUTION

*The electrolyte solution in the battery is a strong and very dangerous acid. It is extremely harmful to the eyes, skin, and clothing. If acid contacts any part of the body it should be flushed immediately with water for a period of not less than 15 minutes. If acid is accidentally swallowed, a person should drink large quantities of milk or water, followed by Milk of Magnesia, a beaten raw egg or vegetable oil. Then contact a physician immediately.*

---

If you must, use a screw type terminal puller (which can be bought in auto parts stores), or spread the cable terminals slightly with a screwdriver then lift up.

Clean any corrosion or acid build-up on the cables, battery case or hold-downs, and inspect them to make sure that they are operating properly, particularly, the hold-downs.

Baking soda, when used with warm water and a stiff cleaning brush, will do an adequate job of neutralizing corrosion and battery acid.

Install the battery in position making sure it sits level. Then tighten the hold-downs a little at a time, alternately, to avoid distorting and breaking the battery cover. Clean the battery posts bright with sandpaper or use a wire brush. Don't hammer the terminals down on the new battery posts; spread them if necessary, and install the starter (positive) cable first and the negative cable (ground) cable last. Tighten the terminal bolts after making sure the cables are not overly stretched or rub against the hold-down or battery cover.

The hold-downs should be snug enough to prevent the battery from bouncing in its frame. Paint or grease (white grease or acid-proof paint) the hold-downs after you have installed them onto the new battery. A small piece of felt under the terminals will help serve as an acid and moisture sponge.

---

# JUMP STARTING

Be very careful when connecting or disconnecting jumper (booster) leads or cable clamps from battery chargers. Make sure that live (working) circuits are disconnected before connecting or disconnecting the booster leads or cable clamps. Faulty connections on the jumper or booster wire (torn or worn insulation) are the most common cause for battery explosions; this is due to electrical arcing. Jumping sparks can ignite a battery and cause a terrific explosion, sending plastic battery material flying like missiles.

For drivers who find themselves with a stalled or dead battery some precautions should be followed to insure a safe and successful jump start. They are:

1. First, be sure that the ignition key is in the off position and all the accessories and lights are off.
2. Shield your eyes if possible. Use goggles or similar eye protection. Sun glasses can serve as a substitute.
3. Connect the jumper cables from the positive (+) battery terminal of the discharged battery to the positive terminal of the vehicle used as the jumper.
4. Connect one end of the other cable to the negative terminal of the good battery.
5. Connect one end of the other cable to an engine bolt head or similar good ground contact on the vehicle being started— not to the dead battery itself.
6. Start discharged vehicle.
7. Carefully remove jumper cables one at a time while discharged vehicle is running, making sure not to touch the cable ends together or to the surface of either car.

## STARTERS

A starter has a pretty tough job. Its job is to spin the *flywheel*, a round disc with teeth bolted to the crankshaft of your engine. When the starter spins the flywheel, the engine turns over. One of the most common errors on the part of both customers and inexperienced mechanics is to assume a starting problem is caused by a bad battery when in fact it is the starter motor. A worn starter motor, after continued use, will crank slower or turn with more difficulty. This draws additional energy from the battery, wearing it down to a discharged condition.

Continually trying to restart a vehicle with a worn starter, or jumping a vehicle with a worn starter motor, is likely to damage the battery internally due to overload and heat.

If a starter motor still cranks slowly with a booster jump it is an indication that the starter, and not the battery, is at fault. Attempting to start vehicles with worn starter motors does not always ruin the battery. After a new starter is installed, usually the battery can be slow charged back to its original optimum condition.

Headlights that are bright coupled with a slow cranking starter usually indicates a problem with the starter and not the battery.

It is needless to explain the inner workings of the starter because starters aren't replaced piecemeal, you have to purchase the whole she-bang. They are seldom rebuilt at customer request, and when they are reconditioned, it is usually done by a machine shop that performs this work in the interest of reselling the rebuilt products back to the retail and parts outlets. That's why there is often a *core exchange policy*, meaning you have to give the facility your old starter in order to get a new one, when a new starter is replaced in your vehicle.

## DIAGNOSING

Since the starter motor is such an essential part of the electrical system, and because it is too easy to fall prey to the mechanic's recommendation that it be replaced, you should be familiar with some symptoms of failure. Some of the symptoms are progressive and give warning before there is a complete component failure in the starter motor. With the following we will examine some of the most common starter and solenoid problems. If your mechanic performs a thorough check and comes up with one of these reasons, then chances are he's on the up and up.

**Nothing Happens When Key Is Turned**—This could mean several things. It could mean the battery is defective or undercharged, or it might be just that the cables are heavily corroded or loose at the terminal. Open the hood of your car and check the cables. If they are corroded, get some baking soda mixed with warm water and a brush, then pour it on the corroded battery terminal and brush off the corrosion. Be careful! The corroded goo is acid and will burn your skin. Don't touch it!

Some cars are equipped with fusible links, or fuses installed in the fuse blocks that burn out when abnormal current is encountered; they are cheap protective devices designed to guard against more expensive damage to the other major components. So the problem could be a burned fuse. On the other hand, it could be a loose or unadjusted neutral safety switch. This switch is sometimes located in the shifting lever console of a car equipped with an automatic transmission, or it is connected to the clutch linkage in manual transmission cars. In other words, it prevents you from starting the car when it is in gear. Auto transmissions must be in "Park" or "Neutral" and the clutch must be depressed to the floor or the gear lever set in neutral in a manual transmission in order for the car to start. This switch occasionally malfunctions.

Speaking of switches, the contacts in your ignition switch can also become worn.

**You Hear A Click**—This could also mean a discharged or defective battery or cables, or loose or defective wiring at the starter. The *solenoid* could also be worn. The starter motor might also be frozen.

**Slow Cranking Starter**—This could be an overheated vehicle. More amps are required to start a hot engine and this would slow the rotational speed of the starter motor. Again, the battery might be undercharged or defective, or the battery-to-engine ground could be loose. Finally, the ignition timing could be off.

**Starter Grinds or Clanks**—This could mean the drive gear in the starter is damaged, you hope, because the alternative is that the teeth on the flywheel, located between the engine and the transmission, are worn. Replacing a flywheel falls into the category of major, expensive repair. Of course, the bearings or bushings in the starter could also be worn, allowing excess play. Finally, it could be a simple case of loose or broken starter mounting bolts, which would throw the alignment off between the gears of the starter and flywheel.

If your car develops any of these symptoms, go to a mechanic and explain them to him thoroughly, using the list of possibilities as a guideline. Because of the complexity of this system, the dealership is your best bet. The dealership will most likely charge you a minimal shop charge of .5 or a half-hour labor for troubleshooting electrical problems. However, the fee is usually credited toward the total bill if you have them do the repair.

**What The Mechanic Should Do**—The first thing that a mechanic should do when diagnosing a starter problem is to examine the present condition of the battery with the load or hydrometer tests previously described. Remember to have him fully charge it prior to these tests if the battery is dead.

The charging circuit should be checked out next to see if the alternator is supplying enough charging voltage to the battery. Once the battery and alternator have passed their respective tests and eliminated as culprits, the starter should be tested for its condition and operability. This is assuming that the other fuse and wiring circuits have been ruled out.

By the use of a volt/ammeter testing unit, the mechanic can check the starter directly and determine through a gauge reading how many amps the starter is requiring to perform its function. If he gives you a reading and tells you it's below that recommended by the manufacturer, ask to see that in the manual. A starter requiring more than its original amp rating load is worn or defective. In addition to the above test, several other procedures are recommended, i.e., a field ground circuit test, a starter no-load test, a starter solenoid test and many others. Without these tests and diagnostic gauges and meters, accuracy cannot be attained in discovering the true operability of the starting and charging circuit. If your mechanic doesn't perform any of these tests, and still recommends a new starter, it is possible that you are being set-up for a quick sale.

## NEW VS. REBUILT

If your starter has been positively diagnosed as defective through the use of proper testing procedures, and if a complete starting and charging circuit evaluation was performed, then you can start thinking about replacing the starter. It's up to you if you want a new (expensive) or rebuilt (inexpensive) replacement starter. My advice is to go with a new unit, because the starter is used frequently and has to bear the strain of turning over the engine. Of course, if you're strapped for funds, or perhaps if you don't value your car all that much, then go with the rebuilt unit. But personally I have found that rebuilt or reconditioned starters are substandard as far as quality, operation and durability are concerned.

**Core Exchange**—An auto repair facility usually requires the exchange of your old starter for the new one, which will get you a discount when you trade it in. Make sure you get this deal. Remember also that solenoids are commonly sold as a package deal with a starter (and rightly so), as the solenoid is considered to be part of the core swap as well. Make sure they give you the solenoid.

**Getting Your Own Part**—Find a special deal on a starter? Fine. But they are difficult to install by yourself unless you're pretty handy with tools. Starters aren't a bonus or commission job, so mechanics don't benefit. However, the shop usually realizes a large profit by overcharging you for the starters when they order it from another facility. That's why they like to sell them to you directly, and that's why if you ask them to install yours, they will probably refuse. Before you go rushing off to purchase a starter from somewhere else (and this goes for most other parts purchases) call the repair shop and tell them what you're doing and ask if they'll install it. That way, you won't be stuck with a starter that sits in your trunk.

## ALTERNATORS

There are many different makes of alternators, but most fall into two basic designs—the standard alternator with a separate regulator and the integrated alternator/regulator single-piece unit. The primary function of the alternator is to recharge the battery and supply electricity to all other systems that require it, only when the engine is running.

## THINGS THAT GO WRONG

When the charging system goes to hell, the idiot light usually comes on in the dash to tell you that the alternator, regulator, or charging circuit wiring is worn or damaged.

**The Belt**—If the alternator belt is loose or has simply snapped, it won't charge the battery. In either case it is a relatively simple chore to tighten the belt or purchase a new one. Even if the belt is intact and appears to be tight, grasping the alternator pulley impeller and trying to turn it will tell you if the belt is loose or slipping.

The belt is adjusted by loosening the alternator bracket and shifting the alternator housing, applying tension on the belt. The belt should be snug and not overly tightened. Make sure you check by looking into the engine compartment for this problem, especially when told by a mechanic that your alternator is frozen and you need a new one. A belt only costs about $7, about 12 times less than an alternator.

**Low Idle**—If the red dash light comes on or is perceivably dim just after you start the car, it is probably due to the decreased rpm's in the engine (low idle). If the red dash light does not disappear after the car is warmed up but does after the accelerator is pushed, it means that the idle speed setting on the carburetor is probably set too low, and this can be remedied by a carburetor adjustment.

These tests are rudimentary and not designed to establish the exact cause of the discharge condition. They are proof enough to know that a definite discharge condition exists. Any vehicle exhibiting such a condition should be taken into a repair facility where the exact and proper diagnosis can be made. The mechanic will make the necessary tests using a volt/ammeter to determine just what the low and high speed voltage output is of the alternator.

## REPLACEMENT

Some parts on some alternators are replaced rather easily. Brushes, for example, are sometimes accessible from the outside of the alternator and cost less than $10 to replace. A mechanic can pop them out, see if they are worn, then put in a new set.

But generally, it is common practice to replace the entire unit. The reason is because the time and labor involved in rebuilding an alternator can equal or exceed the cost of a new one. Like batteries and starters, alternators have a core value and many shops require your old alternator in exchange for a new or rebuilt unit. Unlike starters, a rebuilt alternator is generally adequate, so you don't have to spring for a new one.

## OTHER ELECTRICAL GREMLINS

If your major charging circuit components are checking out and you still have a discharge condition, the problem might lie in the wiring harness, fuse block, or other related wiring circuit. The only facility that does a fairly decent job of troubleshooting a wiring short or other systems fault is a dealership. Most other repair facilities do not have the time, skill and specific wiring diagrams to trace down an elusive wiring problem. Accurate and quick troubleshooting is dependent on the skill and training of the technician, and that is why the dealership is the best bet. Some dealerships may even have an electrical specialist. A dealership technician is more apt to find the problem faster and have the necessary manuals and tools to do the repair work.

It is true that the cost from a dealership will be higher, but that cost could be superseded by another facility that does not know how to handle the problem but instead attempts the repairs, fails, tries again and never succeeds in finding the fault.

> The "maintenance free" battery has many advantages over the non-sealed battery; it holds a charge longer and can withstand prolonged high energy demands, and often comes with a longer warranty. The higher price is worth it.

> A higher rating capacity battery is advised if the energy demands for a vehicle surpass normal operation.

This includes additional aftermarket accessories that have been installed on the vehicle which drive the energy demand up. (Consult owner's manual for battery limitations).

✔ A battery can discharge if an accessory is left on, by a broken alternator belt, by physical damage, loose or corroded cables, low alternator output, high resistance in the charging circuit, a defective starter and sitting for very long periods without activity.

✔ Purchasing an undersized (below rating) battery can result in poor performance and early failure.

✔ Extremely hot or cold conditions can reduce a battery's effectiveness by up to 45%.

✔ Oversized (above capacity rating) batteries should be considered if the vehicle is permanently equipped with numerous aftermarket accessories.

✔ Overcranking should be avoided at all times. Extended attempts to start the engine for more than 30 seconds at a time could result in permanent battery or starter damage. Wait and allow for cool down intervals.

✔ Battery oversell is a reality. It happens when a mechanic does not follow recommended troubleshooting procedures when checking out the entire starting and charging system. Load tests should only be performed on fully charged batteries. Hydrometer tests can be performed on non-sealed batteries, however this battery should also be fully charged before the test.

✔ Slow charging is the best way to bring a battery back up to normal condition. Fast charging, especially on a used or older battery, can weaken or ruin it.

✔ Use extreme caution when installing your own battery. Remember that most repair facilities provide this service free with a battery purchase. If you must install a battery yourself reread the precautions in this chapter.

✔ Starter motors can be internally damaged by prolonged cranking just like batteries. Allow sufficient cool down periods between starting attempts.

✔ The mechanic should check out the battery and charging system when diagnosing a faulty starter.

✔ Headlights that are bright coupled with a slow cranking starter usually indicate a problem with the starter and not the battery.

✔ Overheated engines, loose starter cables, broken engine parts and discharged batteries can appear to look like a starter problem, when in fact they are not. A bad ignition switch, blown starting circuit fuse, defective fuse block, or misaligned neutral safety switch are also unrelated to a bad starter.

✔ High wire resistance and improperly set ignition timing can cause a good starter to crank slowly.

✔ If the starter keeps running after the key is released, it's probably a defective ignition switch or solenoid.

✔ An improperly tuned engine can cause hard starting and should not be mistaken for a bad starter.

✔ Purchasing a new starter is preferred over a rebuilt one. Remember that you have a choice.

✔ If you have a carry-in starter (your own), you can ask the management if they will install it for you for a labor only cost. Some shops do, others don't.

✔ Most alternators today are integrated; both the alternator and regulator are one piece units.

✔ The alternator/regulator maintains appropriate current to the battery and other systems that require it during engine running.

✔ Abnormal readings on a dash amp meter (very high and low) and the red warning light, are the most obvious devices by which a person can tell if he has a discharge condition in the alternator.

✔ Slipping or broken belts, low idle, loose harness wires and a defective regulator device, can all cause discharge conditions.

✔ A discharging alternator/regulator can eventually lead to a no-start condition. The battery needs optimum current from the alternator to supply sufficient energy to the starter motor to turn the engine.

✔ Alternators, starters and generators (if so equipped), have a core value with most repair shops. If you retain your old part chances are the price of a new or rebuilt one will be higher because the shop wants the old part in trade.

✔ Very difficult wiring shorts are best checked out and repaired by a dealership. Typical R & R shops are not equipped to handle this type of technical repair.

# 9

# THE TUNE-UP
## SHATTERING THE MYTH

The auto repair customer is often shammed during a basic and/or major tune-up. Actually, a tune-up is not a repair so much as it is a *preventive maintenance*—a service which restores a vehicle to a state of maximum efficiency for the purpose of maintaining good performance and fuel economy. The term "tune-up" has become synonymous with duty, as though it were a true test of the vehicle owner's dedication and responsibility. To many, it is something that must be done on a strict and regular basis, and it is perceived to be a cure-all for whatever ails your car. It is a catch phrase that promises everything will be just fine after it is performed. Many of you purchase a tune-up without really knowing what it entails or what it is supposed to include and deliver in standard practice. The tune-up is the scapegoat of the engine: far too many ills are diagnosed as tune-up problems, and far too many customers sign the work orders prescribing the service.

I've heard of customers who insisted on tune-ups only to find out later that it was another area of their engine that needed repair, and they okayed the additional work with the shrug of a shoulder. Their comments were always the same, "Well, it was about due for a tune-up anyway."

Do the managers or mechanics argue with this reasoning? Of course not, because they have known all along that the average automobile owner believes that any tune-up is a good tune-up; tune-ups are faultless, blameless, they are a recognized, mandatory service. Once that impressive oscilloscope is rolled out onto the tarmac, customers think that this mysterious machine will somehow make everything all right. Therefore, customers often oversell *themselves* a tune-up. The mechanics just agree, perform the work, find the real problem and collect more money.

In this chapter we will venture into the mysterious realm of the tune-up and discover just what it is, why it is needed and how often it should be performed.

## WHEN SHOULD YOU TUNE-UP?

The two most important reasons for a tune-up are to maintain fuel economy and engine performance. Certainly, the more efficiently an engine performs, the less fuel it will need. Reliability is also enhanced.

Like moths to flames, customers flock to the outlet that is running that advertised coupon special, and sign up for the work believing that they just received a whopping discount. What they fail to consider is that their vehicle might have just had a tune-up some six months or 6,000 miles back. This kind of tune-up would be even premature for a car equipped with standard ignition (the older breaker points and condenser system). If they had an HEI (high energy ignition) system, and tuned up after just 6,000 miles since the last one, the decision could conceivably be 25,000 miles, or two years premature! Can a car equipped with modern electronic ignition go 20,000 miles before a tune-up is needed? You bet it can! Although the average is somewhat lower, the point is that vehicle owners who have been accustomed to tuning their vehicles much more frequently with older ignition systems still believe that this is the correct schedule to adhere to when their vehicles are equipped with present day electronic ignition.

**Bad Gas**—Have you ever pulled out of a gas station with a full tank of gas and discovered that your car is running rough? Don't rush down the street for a tune-up—it just might be some bad gas. Bad, or contaminated gasoline is the probable result of water that has seeped into the underground holding tanks. When that water gets into your fuel tank, your engine will run rough until it evaporates or is used. There are special fuel additives you can buy to remedy this problem.

## ADVANTAGES

What are the plus sides to overly frequent tune-ups? Your engine will run efficiently and smoothly with more reliability. You might save money in the long run because you'll keep the fuel economy up. A major spark plug manufacturer did a survey of over 6,000 cars nationwide. They found that a tune-up, on cars that needed one, increased fuel economy by over 11%. Replacing worn spark plugs alone accounted for a 3% increase. The same test revealed that eight out of every ten vehicles will have some maintenance deficiency that will directly affect fuel economy, emissions or performance. The best guideline is your owner's manual. It is best to follow the recommended intervals for tune-ups suggested by the manufacturer.

## STANDARD VS. ELECTRONIC IGNITIONS

Standard ignition refers to the older type ignition system used on older model cars. The parts involved in a tune-up on these cars consist of breaker points, condenser, spark plugs, rotor and sometimes the distributor cap.

On standard ignitions, the replacement of these parts and a carburetor and timing adjustment, would be considered a minor or standard tune-up. It is the minor tune-up that is most frequently performed nowadays. On standard ignition-type cars, this service would ordinarily be performed about every 8,000 to 12,000 miles, perhaps 15,000 miles if the driving conditions are moderate.

Electronic ignitions, on the other hand, are much more sophisticated and require a different type of tune-up. Electronic ignitions are almost standard on all cars built within the last decade or so. We'll discuss both types of ignitions, and the procedures involved in tune-ups for both.

### A MAJOR STANDARD TUNE-UP

Every shop has its definition of what constitutes a major tune-up, and you'd be well advised to call around to make sure you find one that offers the most service for the best price. I will list the chores and parts normally associated with maximum service. That would include: points (if so equipped), distributor cap, rotor, condenser, replacement of all spark plug wires, PCV valve (if so equipped), PCV filter (if so equipped), complete carburetor and timing adjustment, air cleaner element, valve adjustment (if equipped with solid lifters), fuel filter (carburetor and inline) and any emission control adjustment.

Sometimes a lube, oil and filter are included in a major tune-up price—again, that depends on the facility.

The following is a brief description of the major tune-up elements, their function and some common problems that occur with them.

## SPARK PLUGS

Actually, the spark plug does not produce a spark but provides a *gap* across which the current can jump or arc. The gap is the distance between the two electrodes—one in the center and one curving over the top of it. This hot spark ignites the air/fuel mixture inside the engine (in an area called the combustion chamber) and this explosion is what produces the power to make your car move. The plug must fire (ignite) thousands of times per minute. If it doesn't, then you have what is known as a miss.

**Wear**—Spark plugs wear in the area directly between the gap, making the gap wider. Then the spark has further to jump, and its response gets sluggish. This is why a high speed miss in the engine is sometimes more noticeable than at idle or low speed.

**Heat Range**—Spark plugs have a heat range, which is the ability of the plug to dissipate heat. The further the plug extends into the engine head (the longer the insulator), the hotter the plug will operate; the shorter the insulator the cooler it will function. A cooler plug will quickly accumulate deposits of oil and carbon since it is not hot enough to burn them off. This results in plug fouling and a direct result is sporadic or complete misfiring. On the other hand, a plug that has too high a heat range will burn away the electrode contacts quickly, and sometimes cause pinging or knocking which is formally known as detonation. This can lead to serious engine failure.

Generally, if most of your driving is long distance, at high speed, a cooler range plug is preferred while if most of your driving is stop and go in city traffic, a hotter range is desired. Most new cars with original equipment plugs are of a medium heat range capability, affording a compromise between the two extremes. What most people do not realize is that they can actively choose which heat range best suits their driving conditions. The heat range marking can be found written on the spark plug body. Generally, higher numbers indicate higher heat ranges; lower numbers, lower ranges. There are spark plug charts available that indicate these heat range sizes.

**Inspection**—It is a relatively simple matter to check the condition of your spark plugs by removing them one at a time and inspecting them for wear and discoloration. If that turns you off, at least you should be familiar with the visual signs so you won't be misled when the mechanic shows you "fouled plugs." You can also get an idea of the condition of your internal engine parts.

Normal plugs have a specified gap measured in thousandths of an inch. This increment can be found by sliding a gap or feeler gauge of the same size as the gap specified by your car's manufacturer, in between the electrodes. A snug fit of the gauge (according to specifications) is desirable. The adjustment can be made to narrow the gap by bending the tang of the upper electrode down toward the center electrode, or bending it up to increase the gap.

The visual appearance of the plug is just as important as the gap. The end electrodes on a plug, in a normal condition, will appear a tannish or gray color with perhaps a little electrode wear. It might show signs of slight crust or brownish deposits but this can be considered normal. Assuming that the vehicle is running normally, the coloration is right and the gap is sufficiently set, a plug like this would be considered in good shape and firing properly.

The effects of extremely high temperatures or incorrect heat range can be seen on a plug as a white or blistered insulator. This can also show up as excessive or premature wear on the insulator due to heat. It can be the result of improperly set ignition timing, a low cooling system, a lean carburetor condition or a leaking intake manifold (which allows too much air into the fuel mixture).

If all the other systems are in proper working order, and the plugs still exhibit an overheated or blistered condition, then it would be wise to exchange the plugs with a set a heat range colder.

If the firing end of the plug is covered with a wet and oily coating, it usually indicates oil deposits. More than ever, oil-fouled plugs are found in engines that have a high amount of wear or a mechanical malfunction.

Oil that has reached the plug has done so by passing the piston rings, valve guides, or possibly a blown head gasket. Remember that when any car has oil-fouled plugs it means that a certain amount of oil is passing through the exhaust (being burned by combustion) and if that is the case, you'll often see blue smoke puffing out the rear of the car.

The installation of a hotter range plug can sometimes remedy the fouling problem; only this method is temporary until the defective parts are replaced (the rings, valve guides, etc.)

Carbon-fouled plugs are identified by the presence of dry, soft, black, sooty deposits on the electrodes. Carbon-fouled plugs are typical in cars subject to continuous stop-and-go city driving. Assuming that the plug heat range is correct, carbon-fouling can be caused by a rich fuel mixture (carburetor or fuel injector malfunction), sticking choke, abnormal fuel pump pressure, clogged air cleaner, retarded ignition timing, or overall low cylinder compression. If one or two plugs are badly carbon-fouled, check the condition of the respective plug wires for cracks and bare wire. (A noticeable engine miss can carbon-foul the defective plug). Also look for cracks in the distributor cap between the towers of the affected cylinders i.e., plug number one, two, three, etc.

Carbon-fouled plugs can be easily cleaned and regapped; there is no need to replace them unless the electrodes are obviously worn.

Detonation (pinging) is usually characterized by a broken plug insulator (the ceramic material surrounding the center electrode). Detonation can also be the result of over-advanced ignition timing, inferior gasoline (low octane), a lean air/fuel mixture (carburetion or fuel injection malfunction), engine lugging (very slow driving), or a non-standard application of engine components that boost the compression ratio causing chamber deposits.

Sometimes the excessive use of gasoline additives can cause ash or lead deposits on the spark plugs. It can be seen as light brown or white colored deposits crusted on the side or center electrodes. The plug may even appear to be rusty looking. Normally this condition is harmless, though excess build-up can cause misfiring. Ash-fouled plugs can be cleaned, gapped and reinstalled.

A plug that shows a rusty material build-up, frequently appearing muddy or wet, indicates water that has passed into the cylinder via a blown head gasket or cracked water jacket. The major component should be repaired and the plug replaced since such rust accumulation is very hard to remove. Such a fouled plug would cause a noticeable miss in the affected cylinder.

## DISTRIBUTOR

You can easily check the condition of your distributor cap yourself. This is done by removing the retaining screws (usually two), or the spring clips that hold it (there is no need to take the plug wires off the cap.) Depending on the number of cylinders in the engine, there are metal poles on the upper inside of the cap. They should be inspected for accumulations of carbon and rust, then sanded lightly to clean the surface. The metal pole in the middle (rotor contact pole) should be examined for cracks and burn marks; it can be scraped lightly with a fingernail file to improve its contact surface. The inside of the cap should be wiped with a rag and a bit of alcohol, then scrutinized for hairline cracks (known as carbon cracks). These minute cracks cause shorts and misfiring, and if the cap has them, it should be replaced.

Distributor caps have a habit of misfiring in moist or rainy conditions since moisture can accumulate on the inside of the cap causing shorting and hard-starting. Moisture-laden caps can crack suddenly when they are heated up or they can become brittle in very hot engine compartments.

**Rotor**—Depending upon the make of the car, the rotor will be the plastic knob or disk that sits directly over the distributor shaft. There is no need to remove it but it should be inspected for carbon cracks, and the metal contact can be cleaned like the cap poles.

Be sure to have the rubber "O" ring on the underside of the distributor cap replaced (if so equipped) before the cap is reinstalled. Do not over-tighten the distributor mounting screws and in the case of the snap clip variety, make sure that both clips are snug and snapped into their grooves.

**Points**—Typical of standard ignition is a set of ignition points and a condenser located on the distributor just under the rotor. The points either have a fixed gap (factory preset) or they can be adjusted in thousandths-of-an-inch.

By using a small screwdriver or pick, the points can be opened. The inside surface of the small contact disks should be relatively clean and smooth with no burn marks, pitting, or corrosion. The disks might have a slight sooty appearance and this can be etched away with a small fingernail file. When the contact points are closed the two opposing breaker contacts should be flush and aligned properly. If not meeting flush, the points could be sprung or out of adjustment or a bad distributor part might be the cause. If the points are adjustable, loosening the retaining screws can misalign them and change the gap (dwell degrees). The engine probably wouldn't start because the firing sequence is disrupted. Thereafter they would have to be reset (regapped) to the manufacturer's specification.

**Condenser**—The condenser can be either internally mounted (next to the points) or externally mounted somewhere on the distributor body. It is a small cylinder about the size of a nickel in radius and about an inch long. It has a small wire leading from it that is attached to the terminal on the distributor. It stores electrical energy and blocks the flow of direct current. It works in conjunction with the points and is always replaced along with the points in a minor or major tune-up. A visual inspection of it can tell you little, if anything. It is usually diagnosed, along with the condition of the points, on an oscilloscope.

## SPARK PLUG WIRES

Plug wires rarely last the life of a vehicle. They become rotted, burned, frayed and damaged by other means. Defective wires will cause misfiring by permitting the high tension ignition current to jump through damaged insulation to some part of the engine. In many cases the sound of a "snap" or repeated "clicking" noise of the jumping spark can be heard when there's a break in the wire. Damaged plug wires that arc against another part of the engine can be seen in a darkened garage or at night with the hood up. The jumping spark will be seen as a miniature blue/white lightning bolt, accompanied by a snapping or clicking noise.

Overheating in any wire over a long period of time can cause increased resistance and lead to misfiring. Mechanics can routinely check the resistance in plug wires by the use of an oscilloscope—this is done by examining the length of the firing line that appears on the screen.

One point can be argued against replacing the entire set of plug wires, and that is if only one wire is found to be faulty. You may request that only the bad wire be replaced; individual wires can be cut and custom-fit as a replacement. However, if your car has over 50,000 miles, and if the wires have never been replaced, it would be wise to replace the entire set because the other plug wires might be approaching a similar deteriorating condition. On a new vehicle, replacing one plug wire would certainly be justified.

## PCV VALVE

The PCV valve is a device that allows amounts of burned exhaust gases to pass back through the fuel intake system for the purpose of being recycled. The valve has a ball check in it that frequently becomes stuck due to carbonized gum. It has to be cleaned or replaced regularly, preferably cleaned, since it is designed for permanent maintenance. On the other end of the PCV tube, attached to the inside of the air cleaner, is the PCV filter. The filter keeps most of the heavy burned exhaust gases from entering directly into the throat of the carburetor. It is a small fiber-like sponge and very inexpensive to replace.

## FUEL FILTERS

Fuel filters have the same job as the air filter only they are designed to screen out rust, debris and other foreign particles in the fuel. When fuel filters become clogged, fuel delivery from the gas tank to the engine slows down. When this happens the engine "starves out," stalling or quitting altogether. A general indication that a fuel filter is clogged is when your car bucks and cuts in and out as the engine runs momentarily out of gas. Congested fuel filters can also cause extreme back-pressure to build up in the fuel lines, leading to leaks that could ignite in the engine compartment. Fuel filters are not expensive and should be replaced routinely—every other minor tune-up or so. If you experience any of the above conditions, check the fuel filter first before you are sold a major tune-up.

## AIR FILTER

The air filter should be replaced in a minor or major tune-up, although it may not need it every time. By removing the filter and shining a flashlight or bulb inside the ring, you'll be able to see how clogged it is; if light shines through most of the filament it does not have to be replaced.

If you drive on a lot of dirt roads or in the desert, you should replace and check the filter more often. A good habit is to rotate the air filter in the case so as to offer a fresh and clean side nearest to the air intake snorkle. This can be done every 5,000 miles and serves to get the most service out of the air filter.

For such a simple and uncomplicated part, the air cleaning element is very important to engine performance. A clogged or dirty air filter richens the air/fuel mixture (less air or more fuel) and can increase fuel consumption as much as 10%. Tests have revealed that 1/3 of all vehicles operating on the road today have air filters in need of replacement. A dirty air filter that does not allow fresh intake air into the carburetor can lead to hard-starting and engine stalling.

## ADJUSTMENTS

Along with the ignition parts that are commonly replaced in a minor standard tune-up there are a few adjustments that the mechanic will or should make. After replacing all parts, he should set the distributor timing, if it is needed, on cars equipped with standard ignitions. This is done with a timing light and takes about five minutes.

The next procedure will be to adjust the carburetor (if your car has one); the air/fuel mixture (lean or rich mixture) is adjusted for best rpm idle according to manufacturer's specification.

The very last setting will be that of the idle speed. This the specified setting of the engine rpm's at idle while in park or neutral, and in drive with the brake applied. The settings are specified by the manufacturer.

So what we have here are the parts and adjustments normally associated with a major tune-up on a vehicle equipped with standard ignition.

## WHAT THE MECHANIC SHOULD DO

A mechanic should replace all the spark plugs making sure that they are properly gapped; install a new set of breaker points and condenser, making sure that the points are adjusted; replace the rotor (which can be a push-fit type or screw-on type); then make the normal adjustment of the timing and carburetor. This procedure is quite easy and should not take more than an hour-and-a half—two hours tops.

## ELECTRONIC IGNITIONS

Electronic ignition systems have been around since the mid-1970s. They have become standard equipment on U.S.-built cars, and most of the foreign makes now carry this type of ignition system. You probably have electronic ignition in your car now. It is nearly maintenance-free aside from some components that are replaced due to electrical shorts or wear. The problem is too many people are unaware of this fact and are sold service usually required with a standard ignition tune-up. What they don't realize it that this service is not necessary, or even possible, with an electronic ignition tune-up.

Along with the increased proficiency of new spark plug designs, electronic ignition systems can extend the life of a tune-up threefold. There are several system types in use today. Except for physical appearance, parts placement and the names used used to identify different components, there is surprisingly little change from one system to another.

## TROUBLESHOOTING

There is a lot that can go wrong with electronic ignition, but this doesn't happen as frequently as one would think. Troubleshooting electronic ignition components is very difficult for the layman or backyard mechanic.

It always requires a test scope to determine and pinpoint such faults in a system of this design. A qualified mechanic must use several procedures or "go, no go" operations to find a faulty part. An engine can miss, die, or not start at all when a major component in the electronic ignition system is at fault. If an engine will not start at all, it is a good bet that the fault lies with either the carburetor or the electronic ignition system. But I have seen electronic systems last over 60,000 miles of operation. In several cases owners have claimed that they have never had a part replaced in this system except for spark plugs. On most cars with electronic ignition, I've seen the distributor cap replaced more often than any other internal part. And even this is not as necessary a replacement procedure as it is with standard ignition.

So what do we have here? Well, we have a nearly fail-safe system (as opposed to the old standard type) that is durable and seldom breaks down. When it does, it is affordably replaced or repaired.

## MINOR ELECTRONIC TUNE-UP

The electronic tune-up should be comprised of everything that is included in the minor standard tune-up, minus a few parts.

However, all standard adjustments should be included: timing, carburetor (mixture and idle), a fast idle choke adjustment, or any other necessary carburetor adjustment. If your car has electronic fuel injection, then this should be adjusted and checked as well. A mechanic should know, via the pattern on the oscilloscope, whether your electronic ignition components are in proper working order, as well as the condition of your plug wires, vacuum lines, coil output, battery and charging condition. You should always have your spark plugs replaced. It is quite possible, depending upon the repair facility, that a valve adjustment will be part of the minor tune-up, although it is generally part of the major tune-up.

## MAJOR ELECTRONIC TUNE-UP

A major electronic tune-up should include everything in the minor tune-up plus some added services and parts.

The distributor cap should be replaced and a valve adjustment performed. All the necessary carburetor adjustments should be made, unless your car has a sealed or capped system in which the carburetor cannot be adjusted. On a sealed carburetor, it is often necessary to remove the carburetor from the car to take off plastic knobs that have been installed over the adjustment screws, and this service might cost extra.

All filters should be replaced; fuel, air and PCV. Your car might have two fuel filters: one at the carburetor, and an inline canister type filter located between your gas tank and the fuel pump. Filter replacement will depend on what make or type automobile you own.

## FUEL INJECTION & THE COMPUTER

Almost all new cars today have fuel injection. If your car does not have a carburetor, it has a gasoline or diesel engine with a fuel injection system. They are just too complicated to work on for the average layman—even testing the skills of a highly trained mechanic.

**Service**—It's true that fuel injection systems are more costly to repair than carbureted types, but they are here to stay, so you'll have to learn to live with the high price tag charged by dealerships and specialists. As far as service is concerned, my advice is to go to the dealer or a specialist only. The sophistication of these systems is often way beyond the gas station, department or chain store mechanic.

## COMMON TUNE-UP SHAMS

**The Rush Job**—Not all, but some repair mechanics have a nasty little habit of rushing an electronic tune-up. What can happen? It's mostly what doesn't happen and what doesn't get done.

In short, in the case of a small compact car, he could glance at the oscilloscope, screw four spark plugs into it and go for coffee. No adjustments, no inspection, no road test, no valve adjustment, no filter replacements, no cap or other services and so on. You'd pick up the car and drive away none the wiser. How could this be?

Well, it was probably running pretty well when it came in. For instance, the timing was dead on, the carb mixture and idle speed checked out, the firing line (on the scope) looked okay, and it was running smooth enough so a valve adjustment wasn't really necessary. The fluid levels in the engine compartment were close enough so why bother?

It took the mechanic about 10 to 18 minutes to do this tune-up because he buzzed the plugs out with a pneumatic driven wrench and replaced them just as fast.

The scope hook-up took about two minutes flat with about 30 seconds to read three different test patterns. The only adjustment he might have been forced to make would be the idle speed since it would normally change with the inclusion of four new spark plugs. This adjustment would take about three minutes. Elapsed time: about 25 minutes, give or take. What was the repair facilities cost for this tune-up? Maybe $2.00 for all four plugs, around $9.00 for the mechanic's labor. So $11.00 is what their cost is. What was the total on your repair invoice? Anywhere from $80.00 to $150.00. Did you get your money's worth? I don't see how it adds up. After all, you waited all day for your car.

In a shop where mechanics are paid a commission on parts and a bonus for extra cars over a certain quota, this quickie type of tune-up happens often. Replacing just the plugs usually solves a culprit miss, or a rough running engine. New plugs are also great for showing a marked improvement in fuel economy and engine performance.

**Hood-Up Syndrome**—The above example also explains the "hood up" syndrome, a case where you find that your car is left unattended in a stall with the engine hood up and no mechanic can be seen working on it. This is probably due to the fact that the mechanic finished very quickly on your car and wants to leave the impression (in case you check), that there is still something to be done on it. Only he is out of sight working on his next ticket. This facade is very common at dealerships where the customer is known to be waiting nearby for the release of his car.

**Misdiagnosis**—Let's say that you take your older car, (one equipped with a carburetor) into a service center because the engine is running rough (missing), or running sporadically. The mechanic tells the manager that a tune-up will set things right, so the manager gets the okay from you (your signature) on the repair invoice.

Four hours later you get a phone call from the manager who informs you that your car took the tune-up all right, but he recommends that you rebuild or replace the carburetor. In fact, he tells you that a new carburetor (or a rebuilt one) will cost you less than having yours torn down and worked on. His reason for this added repair? He might say that the "carb is on its way out anyway so there wouldn't be any harm in taking care of it now." So he wants your verbal okay over the phone so he can jot down the time of the call and initial it on your invoice. This protects him later in case there is a dispute.

More often than not, the car was misdiagnosed by the mechanic. He mistook a carburetor miss for an ignition miss. They are very similar in symptoms, sometimes impossible to diagnose on the spot without studying the problem at length. In a high volume shop, where tune-ups are a big part of the income, mechanics can rush a diagnosis and pin the problem on a faulty ignition system. And it is true that most engine misses are the result of an ignition miss in the primary or secondary circuits. But then a sputtering carburetor comes along and throws him a curve. He's worried because he just installed tune-up parts in your car. He doesn't want to take them out, so he will now have to cure the real problem (the original error) by fixing or replacing the real culprit—the carburetor.

Not only that, but he informs his manager that he doesn't have the skill to rebuild your carburetor so he suggests a new or rebuilt one. That way he has merely to bolt the replacement carburetor on the manifold.

So you'll be told that you need a whole new carburetor because your old one was faulty. All because the mechanic misdiagnosed the original problem. My advice is to ask the mechanic to demonstrate where your carburetor is really faulty. If it truly is, tell them you'll buy the carburetor if they throw in the tune-up for free. What would be the cost for such a mistake? The price of the tune-up and the additional cost of the carburetor and labor, can run as high as $200.

**Camping Out**—"Camping out," "pitching a tent," or "vacationing" on a car are terms that refer to an instance where a mechanic is diagnostically stuck. Something is wrong and he can't find the problem, so the delay is extreme; several more hours than the job would take, or in some cases, days. So they stall you off somehow; telling you that they are waiting for a "special" part to arrive. In fact, they might justify their tardiness by assuring you that it must be done "absolutely right" and don't you think it should be?

A common scenario would involve a customer who takes a turbocharged, fuel-injected vehicle into a tire store for a system tune-up and the shop does not have the proper equipment to diagnose or repair the system. "Camping out" most often occurs with difficult tune-up related service, where heavy diagnosis must be performed.

**The Sealed Carb Caper**—The older carburetor-equipped vehicles sometimes came with plastic knobs that were fitted over the mixture and idle speed screws. To perform a tune-up mechanics had to remove these caps by simply popping them off so they could make the adjustment, then reinstalling them after the tune-up was finished. Most of these cars, and many today, still have these caps and some are more difficult to take off than others. But the mechanic that tells you he needs to charge you an extra $35 to pull your carburetor completely off the vehicle to get at the caps is pulling a scam. Even though the procedure is recommended by shop repair manuals, every mechanic I know has learned how to do this without pulling the carb. Most of these caps can stay off for good—they are only put there to ward off tampering by an unskilled customer who wants to adjust his own carburetor.

**The Cover Up**—If a mechanic can't tune your car to the point of a smoothly running engine by following the exact tune-up specifications (by the book), he is likely to make a few of his own "hot rod" adjustments to get the car running better. Two of the easiest ways to give a car more power or mask a rough running engine, is too richen the carburetor mixture and advance the timing a few degrees.

This will "cover up" his mistake. And you probably won't know the difference until you try to have a smog check, or check your fuel mileage. You'll fail the smog check, and your fuel mileage will decrease.

Then the bad adjustment would have to be readjusted at extra expense (not to mention a rough running engine that the smog mechanic now has to repair because the original tune-up was botched). Insist that your car be set to "manufacturer's specifications," the condition in which your car was designed to perform at its peak. If the car is set to "specs" and still runs poorly, the mechanic has not done the job properly.

**Mileage From Heaven**—Don't be surprised if you pull out of a service center having just had a tune-up, and discover during the next week that you are getting miraculous gas mileage.

What they have done is overinflate each one of your tires from five to seven pounds (over specifications), to make it appear that their tune-up was so good that you are now saving money because of their superior workmanship. A vehicle's tires can be overinflated without any noticeable wear. Overinflated tires use less friction when rolling over the ground. The instant result is increased fuel economy due to over-inflated tires, not the tune-up.

Do this before a tune-up as a safeguard: check and adjust your tire pressure via your owner's manual recommendation. If after the tune-up your tires are higher in reading, it means that you've been duped. Also, your car might ride a little rougher after this sham has been done. I know of several major tire and department store repair shops who are using this device today. It is one of the newest tricks in their stable!

**Protecting Yourself**—How can you protect yourself and be assured that you are getting maximum service and care? There is a neat little trick that can be used when you visit an auto repair facility for a tune-up, standard or electronic. You simply type or write a list of tune-up procedures you want performed on your car and present them to the mechanic. These request services are actually part of the tune-up, and when the mechanic reads the request list, he will recognize that you are a stickler for detail and thoroughness. The list that works best has empty boxes in the right margin that must be manually checked off by the mechanic. Is this type of "list strategy" out of the ordinary? No. That doesn't mean mechanics like them, but they will usually follow the directions and check off the boxes. What follows is an example of a request list, or what may be termed an "action item list."

1. Compression check.
2. Engine scope and diagnosis.
3. Replace spark plugs and gap new ones.
4. Replace cap, rotor, or other electrical component that is obviously bad.
5. Adjust valves if needed.
6. Check fuel and air filters—replace if needed.
7. Complete carburetor adjustment, idle mixture, speed, choke setting (fast idle).
8. Inspect vacuum lines for wear and leaks.
9. Clean PVC valve.
10. Report spark plug wire continuity.
11. Perform L.O.F. if needed and attach sticker to door jamb.
12. Please road test.
13. Would you please save old parts and bag them. Include guarantee.

signed_____

You can make up your own list that is specially tailored for your particular make and year of automobile. Consult your owner's manual for the prescribed periodic maintenance chores and services. You will hand this list to the manager, who will in turn clip it on the work order invoice. You could tell the manager that you are conscientious about keeping accurate repair and service records on your vehicle because you are thinking about selling or trading in the vehicle and you realize that maintenance documents are in your financial favor when about to sell or trade. The manager will perfectly understand this request because it makes good common sense.

Or you can plainly state that you are a perfectionist (with apology) and would like to have the work done right. Whatever excuse you use, you will find that this list works with a tune-up better than any other auto repair service. Make copies of your list so you can use a fresh one every time.

**Special Deals**—What if you came into a service center for a routine brake inspection or a battery charge and the mechanic told you that you needed a tune-up? What if he says that it's your lucky day because they just happen to be running a special and if you don't take advantage of it now, the price is sure to go up next week? Let's also assume that your tune-up is not due for another 10,000 miles and your engine is presently running as smooth as silk, good fuel economy, etc. Should you take advantage of this incredible one-time offer? I certainly wouldn't. Paying for tune-ups is not like shopping for groceries in which you take advantage of a deal because it is posted, spread by word of mouth, or advertised.

Women should be particularly on their guard with this tactic, because managers like to appeal to their money-saving, bargain-shopping senses and will liken his offer to a K-Mart blue light special that you can't resist.

Managers will prey on a different sense when dealing with a bachelor. Along with the implied "saving money" theme, a manager might try to appeal to a man's need for more power and performance, especially if he has a sports car. If you hear this one, you know you're being had because a tune-up, either major or minor, will not add horsepower or torque to the engine. A tune-up is a maintenance procedure that keeps the engine running at maximum efficiency, at its stock, peak horsepower and torque output. In other words, it just keeps it running as closely as possible to the way it did when it rolled off the showroom floor. Tune-ups are not "modifications," and don't deliver large performance gains. Don't fall for this appeal to your sense of *machismo*.

 Regularly scheduled tune-ups provide the best performance and fuel economy. Regular tune-up service can also ward off breakdowns and car trouble in adverse weather.

✔ Your owner's manual is the best reference source for knowing how often to perform standard or major tune-up service on your car.

✔ Before a tune-up, have the mechanic verify that you actually need one. Make sure that a surge, engine miss, stumble or hesitation is not caused by some other area that can't be fixed with a tune-up. For instance, you might have a vacuum hose disconnected, which is causing an engine surge. Don't automatically ask for a tune-up; ask that they "fix the miss or surge." Try to narrow the problem down instead of generalizing.

✔ Remember that cars with electronic ignition do not have to be tuned as frequently as the older standard ignition models. Some cars can go 30,000 miles and more before an electronic tune-up is needed! Consult your manual.

✔ If you do not adhere strictly to your owner's manual for tune-up schedules, then use some common sense. Trying to stretch every last mile out of a tune-up (procrastination) will eventually produce hard-starting, bad performance in wet weather and poor fuel economy. If you notice any one of these three signs it means that you have gone too far between tune-ups and one is needed.

✔ Find out exactly what is included in a standard or major tune-up from your owner's manual, then compare that list with what a repair facility offers. Go to the facility that most closely follows the guidelines set forth by your owner's manual.

✔ If your spark plugs are being replaced, make sure they are the proper heat range. If your driving habits are exclusively high speed and long distance, a cooler range plug can be used. If you always travel in congested city traffic, a hotter range plug is best.

✔ Remember that old spark plugs can tell a story about what condition your engine is in. Have the mechanic explain to you any abnormal wear pattern or condition of any of your old spark plugs. For instance, an oil-fouled plug warns of excessive oil consumption (internal engine problem).

✔ Use a tune-up list approach when going to a repair shop for a tune-up. Make sure the manager takes the list and passes it off to his mechanic.

✔ For fuel injection service make sure that the repair facility you approach has the proper training and diagnostic equipment to do the work properly. Department stores and quick stops are not good candidates for this service—go to dealerships and specialty shops who employ mechanics certified in this area of repair. Do not attempt to work on fuel injection systems yourself.

✔ The Association of Diesel Specialists do work exclusively on Diesel cars. They carry the ADS logo and their mechanics are certified for diesel work. This is the only place to take your diesel powered vehicle if you are unsure of the proper repair facility.

✔ If you can, stay around and watch and monitor the tune-up. Presenting a face with the car works very well with tune-up service. Your visual presence keeps mechanics on their toes and less likely to pull sneaky scams.

# 10

# THE SMOG CHECK

## A DREADED ENIGMA

If you don't have mandatory emission control (smog) checks in your state, you will soon. The pollution caused by the daily emission of tons of hydrocarbons, carbon monoxide and oxides of nitrogen into our atmosphere is a phenomenon no longer limited to California, which has the most stringent emission control policies in the country. Real hard facts of acid rain, the greenhouse effect and the destruction of our ozone are prompting the federal government to get involved. Many states have already adopted California's air quality control policies.

So the smog check is here to stay, and because it is a mandatory repair service, it is prone to dishonesty. Smog checks have not been around for a very long time, but there have been more lawsuits and more complaints filed with the California Bureau of Automotive Repair (BAR) with this service (per ratio) than any other.

Because California has the most stringent emission control procedures and most states are adopting these procedures, most of what I'll talk about applies to this state. Some of the procedures and legalities may differ where you live, but you'll get the basic idea of what's involved and what's not involved, in a basic smog check.

# EMISSION CONTROL FUNCTION

There are three major types of exhaust gas pollutants given off by the internal combustion engine: hydrocarbons (HC), carbon monoxide (CO), and oxides of nitrogen (NOx).

It is the function of the various emission control devices installed on your vehicle to reduce the amount of HC, CO, and NOx emissions reaching the atmosphere as much as possible. Emission control devices can do this by limiting their formation during combustion, or by neutralizing them after they have formed. For example, spark retard and EGR (exhaust gas recirculation) systems help prevent the formation of CO and NOx to promote more complete combustion of HC.

Various "afterburner" devices such as the air injection system and the catalytic converter, work by burning up any residual HC and CO after they have formed in the combustion chamber but before they exit the exhaust.

# THE INSPECTION

In California, a car must be smog checked every other year when it is time to be re-registered. Owners are required to submit proof of a smog check before they receive their tags, unless the car is deemed exempt, or the cost of repairs exceeds a preset limit. Smog inspections are also required whenever there is a transfer of ownership with a vehicle.

---

### HINT

*If you've recently swapped or replaced your engine, you are required to tell the mechanic this before the smog check is performed. He is supposed to refer you to the nearest California Bureau of Automotive Repair office for authorization and referee intervention. You'll have to bring all of your paper work to verify the source of the new engine and date of installation. The referee station then has the option of "approving" or "disproving" the engine, making sure it complies with the original manufacturer's emission control components and operability. If it fails, they'll tell you what needs to be done to bring it up to specs. Once you do that, it can be retested.*

---

**Initial Inspection**—Smog check stations are so designated by the state and issued a license after complying with tests and regulations. When you first arrive for the smog check, your car is given a visual inspection just to make sure all emission devices are still on the car and secured properly. This inspection is prior to the actual test, before any analysis or adjustments are made. If anything is missing, such as belts, or vacuum hoses, you'll be told that the condition or problem has to be fixed before the test. And, of course, they'd be willing to fix it for you. Following are some of the emission control systems and components for which a licensed mechanic will visually check to determine if they have been disconnected, missing, or modified:

1. Positive Crankcase Ventilation (PCV)
2. Thermostatic Air Cleaner (TAC)
3. Air Injection (AI)
4. Fuel Evaporation System (FE)
5. Fill pipe Restrictor (Gas Nozzle)
6. Catalytic Converter (Oxidizing Catalyst)
7. Three-Way Catalytic Converter (TWC)
8. Exhaust Gas Recirculation (EGR)
9. Spark Advance Controls
10. Computer Controlled System (CCS)
11. Fuel Injection Controls
12. Retrofit Devices

Next the mechanic will enter the year model of your car, its engine size and number of cylinders into a test analyzer. For 1972 and newer vehicles, he will look at the under-hood emission control label. Both California and federal laws require that every new vehicle have a permanent label in the engine compartment containing: the name of manufacturer; vehicle conformity (U.S. EPA) emission control requirements; engine size in cubic inches, liters or cc's; emission control type; engine tune-up specifications; and adjustments recommended by the manufacturer. This label is commonly located over the radiator in many cars, or on the fender side panel.

If for some reason the label is missing, obliterated, or difficult to read, the mechanic can refer to an emission control system application manual that will have this information along with the necessary diagrams.

**Analysis**—Once a vehicle has been visually inspected and has proven to the licensed mechanic that all systems are intact, the next procedure will be to attach the vehicle to an emission exhaust analyzer to test each system for operability and overall function.

This requires the mechanic to insert an exhaust probe, commonly referred to as a "sniffer," into the tailpipe of the vehicle. The sensing device located in the probe and the line that is attached to it relay the condition of the exhaust gases to an exhaust gas analyzer, which determines the precise amounts of chemical emissions from the exhaust and translates this information to the mechanic via a printed readout and/or digital display.

On the readout, emission control components will be listed along with the subsequent reports on those systems. The systems will be marked with either a "pass" or "fail." A "fail" response indicates that a system is malfunctioning, disconnected, or in need of repair. Or that the overall emission gases exceeded the maximum allowable amounts for that year and make automobile.

A percentage reading will accompany the emission results. The following is an example of a typical computer tape readout.

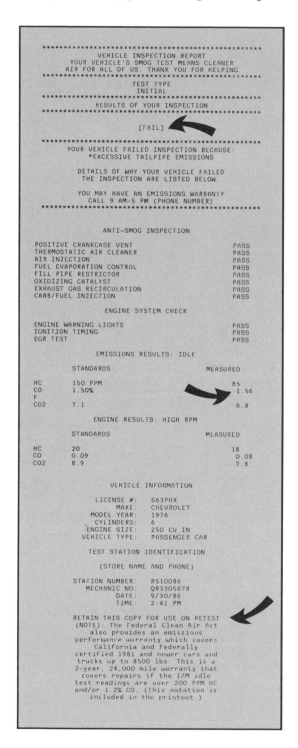

No doubt the test information seems confusing. Under the emission results heading you will notice that this car produced a reading of CO (carbon monoxide) in an amount of 1.56. After the 1.56 reading there is an "F" which denotes a fail. The standard for that car for CO emissions is 1.50% or less, as indicated by the number to the left. Naturally, the car flunked the first smog test. At the very end of the printed readout there is a notation to "RETAIN THIS COPY FOR USE ON RETEST." In other words this car will have to be retested, but first the (idle) emission under the CO heading will have to be adjusted or repaired (In this case an adjustment will have to be made to bring the vehicle within acceptable specifications.)

**Retest**—When the vehicle is tested again it will receive another printout and it will not be unlike the first one aside from some different phrases and the addition of a "REPAIRS PERFORMED" section that will end at the bottom of the list. On the new printout (since it passed this time) will appear the words PASS under the "RESULTS OF YOUR INSPECTION" heading. Beneath that heading will appear "CERTIFICATE OF COMPLIANCE: B4389834" with the positive phrase, "CONGRATULATIONS YOUR VEHICLE PASSED THE CALIFORNIA EMISSIONS INSPECTION." Thanks a lot.

**Cost**—In California, for instance, this first inspection costs around $20 for the test, plus an additional $6 or so for the certificate (paperwork). If our test car had passed the first time, the cost would be around $26 with no additional expense. However, this vehicle failed and had to be repaired/adjusted and then run through the test again.

In California there is a maximum fee for making this and most other adjustments and light repairs to your emission control system. There is a $50 maximum charge for such a second testing and repair/adjustment, which includes the first test fee, which in this case was $26. That means that the mechanic could charge up to $24 more to reach the maximum. And this is where it gets a little bit tricky, especially if you fail and need some type of repair/adjustment.

The cost for the certification and smog check varies from state to state. You will have to check with your local certified smog test and repair station.

**Passing Grades**—Frequently, vehicles that have just had tune-ups prior to a smog inspection pass the tests regularly. If you are ready for a smog inspection, a tune-up plus the replacement of all filters will help your car pass the test. Also, make sure all vacuum lines are routed and tightly fitted to their proper connections. Consult your emission control diagram for proper hook-ups and routing. You can find it in your owner's manual, or the sticker will be prominently displayed in your engine compartment.

**Recertification**—Once a vehicle has passed a smog check from a certain facility, the vehicle owner would be very wise to take that car back to the same facility for any future smog checks. Bringing along the past receipts and smog check printouts is an excellent way for the vehicle owner to show that his car has performed well in the past and has been certified with passing grades. It is a very good time to compare printouts and determine what systems on the vehicle have changed or are beginning to wear.

## COMMON SHAMS

Quite often, you'll see advertisements reading something like "Complete Smog Check $19.95" or my personal favorite, "Pass or Don't Pay." If your car can't be fixed for $50 or less in order for it to pass the test, you will still get a smog certificate. But believe me, unless the problem is major, mechanics will do everything to tune the car to the $50 limit. Then your ticket will run $50, plus the $19.95 and usually $5 for the certificate. However, there are some facilites that advertise "Pass or Don't Pay" that only offer a smog check—period. They'll check your car but they don't repair them or make any adjustments. If you fail the test, you don't owe them a dime. If you pass, you must pay their price. However, they don't work on the car: they are literally a check-only type of business. What you could do is have them run the check, and if it fails, go somewhere else you trust to have your car tuned, then go back for the test.

At least the law is working for you. Every test performed in California is documented, approved by an inspector, logged and turned over to the state for review by the Bureau of Automotive Repair, and other states have similar checks and balances. And the Bureau is always on the lookout for a falsified entry, inaccurate tape, or forged invoice, but they are understaffed and overworked. So if the mechanic does pull a sham he stands a good chance of getting away with it. If he is caught, he could then lose his license. But that threat doesn't stop the dishonest mechanic from employing a few tricks.

## THE SET UP

A mechanic can skirt the legal boundaries of a smog check by just selling you parts ahead of time, telling you that the installation of these parts will help your car pass. Quite often he will do this just after the visual inspection but *before* the initial test. You could be sitting in the waiting room and suddenly the mechanic appears with your invoice. He explains to you that your air cleaner, PCV valve and filter, and a couple of vacuum lines need replacement. On the invoice you might find it written under the heading of "mechanic's recommendations."

Bear in mind now that he hasn't even run your car through the initial

> # CAUTION
>
> *Be most careful during the visual inspection prior to the smog check. A mechanic could insure a "max" on your invoice with a couple of nasty tricks. He could, while doing the visual, disconnect a vacuum line, or turn an air/fuel mixture screw out, which would immediately set the car up for a "fail" or "repair/adjust" reading, as soon as the initial test is performed. He could temporarily disconnect an emission control component with the deftness of Houdini, and if you were not around to watch the operation, you would be none the wiser. I've heard of one mechanic who always kept a clogged PVC valve in his box, and when doing an inspection, he would routinely substitute it for the customer's part, which prompted a fail every time. To repair it, he would reinstall the customer's original functioning PCV valve back onto the system and charge them for a new one nevertheless. Watch the mechanic closely. He should not have to lean into your engine compartment and handle anything, unless it is to test the tautness of a vacuum line. He is justified in touching something when he begins the actual test on the vehicle.*

test, but has in fact given you some immediate recommendations. All too often customers think that these preliminary recommendations are part of or essential to the actual test when they don't really have anything to do with it, since he hasn't tested your car yet.

If you query him as to why you need the parts he might say, "these parts are a good insurance before a smog test." Or "the parts don't look too good and new ones would help the test."

He hasn't said that you will actually fail if you don't follow his recommendations. What he has done is raise a question, provide you with an unanswered mystery: "It just might fail without the part." He could say, " I just don't know about that EGR valve." Whereupon you answer, "Do you think that I should replace it?" His answer will almost always be, "Yes, it's best."

If your car had been smogged, he would have had a tape readout in his hand to show you whether it failed or passed. That would be the proper time to buy the parts or recommended services to correct the failure and insure your certification—when he showed you a failed readout. If you've recently had your car tuned up, then I would be especially suspicious if any of the above happened.

## TWISTING THE SCREW

It's happened before that a mechanic has deliberately set the air/fuel mixture to an overly rich condition during the visual inspection prior to testing the car. One of the best things you can do to protect yourself against this is to observe the mechanic during the visual inspection to make sure he makes no adjustments to the car. He shouldn't even touch it until after he's run the test, especially with a screwdriver.

## COLD TESTING

In order for a smog test to be accurate, the engine must be up to operating temperature. A test given with a cold engine will almost surely fail, because most cars compensate for cold starting by going to an overly rich condition, also known as the choke setting. All other emissions control equipment on the car needs to be up to a specific temperature to function properly. If your car has been sitting for a long time, make sure the mechanic warms it up sufficiently before performing the test. This time period could be as long as 30 minutes.

## NEW CARS

If your car is still covered under its basic warranty, and it fails a smog check, then you should take it back to the dealer. Federal laws require that carmakers ensure their cars are emissions-legal for a period of 5 years. If you aren't aware of this fact, the smog-test mechanic probably won't tell you. For more on warranties, go to the end of chapter 11.

- ✔ The three major types of exhaust gas pollutants given off by the internal combustion engine are: hydrocarbons (HC), carbon monoxide (CO), and oxides of nitrogen (NOx).

- ✔ It is the function of the various emission control devices installed on your car to reduce HC, CO, and NOx emissions. You should maintain your factory installed emission control components for this reason.

- ✔ Smog checks; repair/adjust, and certification can only be done by an officially licensed smog check repair station with a licensed and authorized mechanic performing the adjustments and repairs.

- ✔ For 1972 and newer vehicles, the emission control label is located under-the-hood and displayed in plain sight. If it is not, or has been obliterated, a mechanic can refer to an emission control system application manual.

- ✔ If a mechanic tries to sell you parts after a visual inspection but before a test, tell him to perform the routine check anyway because the tape readout will be the judge of that. A mechanic cannot tamper with the results of the machine; you are assured a fair shake with the analysis.

✔ Make sure your vehicle is brought to full operating temperature before actual testing begins. Cold, or choked engines often fail the smog check. Tell the mechanic to warm it up.

✔ In California, there is a maximum $50.00 cost limit for fixing a failed car. It applies to: adjustments/repairs to lower tailpipe emissions; correction of conditions causing "check engine" lights to be on; repairs to worn-out or defective emission controls that are not missing, modified, or disconnected. It does not apply to a major or minor tune-up.

✔ Is there any way to get a certificate if the emissions still fail the standards after the repair and retest? Yes, if the originally failed emission is reduced and the other emission is still within standards. Or if further repairs will exceed $50.00, then a special certificate can be issued due to exceeding the cost limit. In California, if the emissions cannot be reduced, the vehicle must be referred to the Bureau of Automotive Repair for review. The BAR will retest the vehicle.

✔ A mechanic can refuse to inspect/repair or certify your vehicle if he finds: an obvious oil, transmission, fuel or coolant system leak; if the maintenance warning light is on; a safety problem; an excessive exhaust system leak; an inaccessible exhaust; high or low engine rpm; excessive engine or bearing noise; an unknown certification status. In these instances the problem area or system will have to be repaired by the vehicle owner before a test and certification can be given.

✔ If you own a newer vehicle and your test shows that you have failed, it is possible that a failed part on your car (responsible for the emission failure), is under warranty. In this case, you can ask the advice of the mechanic as to whether a warranty part has gone bad, leading to the failed condition. If so, you can take your vehicle to the new car dealership and have the part replaced, then return to the station for a retest.

# 11

# PROTECT THYSELF

## WHAT TO DO WHEN YOU'VE BEEN RIPPED OFF & TIPS TO SAVE MONEY

The time will come one day when you are confronted with an auto repair bill that defies common sense. Or there will be a time when your vehicle has not been repaired properly or is worse than it was before you brought it in for repair. You could find yourself broken down on some lonely stretch of highway that is nothing more than a rabbit trail on the map, way out in Boonesville, and your only hope of salvation comes from some greasy shyster in a grimy service station truck. There will be other times when you are in a jam and need your car and the mechanic has you over a barrel with an outrageous repair bill. And there will be times when an estimate will make you feel ill, wondering if your car is worth the expense of repair. Don't panic; try a few things first.

## FAIR EXPENSE

If you are in a shop and the repair cost seems high (which is almost always the case), you can ask the manager to check his shop labor cost manual, or his flat rate manual, to find out what the book says about tear-down and repair time. Or if you see that the actual repair time (from start to finish) conflicts with the labor costs they have marked on their labor cost placard, tell this to the service manager, stating how much time you witnessed the job to take. Sometimes the labor cost or flat rate book indicates a specific labor time for a particular job, only many mechanics "beat" this time and finish the job in half the time period. (This is very common since tools are much improved and mechanics work much faster than they once did.) However, you will still be charged for the full rate stated in the flat rate manual. This leads to what is known as the "hood-up" syndrome. This is a scam where a mechanic finishes the repair early, but leaves the hood up or your car on the lift the entire time to give you the impression they are still working on it. You should rightfully insist, for example, that if you're being charged for 1.8 hours of labor time to perform the job, then the mechanic should spend that entire block of time on your brake system if he finished early. Either that, or you should only be charged for the actual time spent on the car, and not the time set by a self-serving flat rate manual.

## FALSE OBLIGATION

Many customers feel they are obligated to follow through with a recommended repair once their car has been torn down or visually inspected. This show of "good faith," especially if it is with a first-choice shop, is needless. You might say, "but they took the time to find the problem, and for nothing! So why shouldn't I show them that I trust their judgment?" My answer to that is to find out the charge before you cough up so much loyalty. Generally, a repair estimate over $150 for most remove and replace work should convince you to start thinking logically instead of emotionally. Can you get a better deal down the street? Would the parts be cheaper? What is the flat rate labor charge at the other shop? Would the diagnosis even be the same? Are the mechanics more qualified at the other facility? These questions are relevant to second opinions, and if you are thinking like this you are on the right track.

## USING THE RIGHT CHANNELS

If anything can dissuade you from a physical fight, hollering match, shoving contest, temper tantrum, tears, or any other sign of emotional aggression or deterioration, LET IT! Don't get into a row, or heated disagreement with the repair staff if you feel that you have been mugged by Mr. Bum Wrench. If you haven't paid the bill yet, and you refuse to pay it, you have several options.

## THE BAR

If you live in California, you can call the Bureau of Automotive Repair (BAR). The number should be displayed right there in the service center. Just by saying so, you might scare the manager or mechanic into re-examining the repair order and within seconds it will be reduced. That's when you know they've been shining you on.

But if that doesn't happen, call the local BAR and ask an operator or referee what to do. He, or she, will probably tell you to pay the bill anyway and report to the office immediately, or set up a date for an appointment. If you don't pay your bill, remember that the facility has your car keys and you won't be able to leave the premises.

The BAR office will have you fill out a form and explain all the details of the work that was performed on your vehicle. Be certain to bring all of your receipts and anything related to the case as evidence to the BAR office. After an extensive review, they will make a decision to either deny your claims that you've been ripped off, or they will intervene and serve as an intermediary between you and the repair shop for the purpose of refunding your money, or reaching a compromise for both parties concerned.

## THE BBB

While you are at it, you could also telephone the Better Business Bureau (BBB) and explain your case to them. They can look up the records of the shop and determine how many complaints have been logged with them in the past, whether the cases were resolved and what kind of attitude the shop had in treating its customers. This information from the Better Business Bureau would be secondary ammunition that you could take to the Bureau of Automotive Repair.

## OFF TO COURT

If you are unsatisfied with the results of the BAR or the BBB, you can file for a small claims suit and proceed to take the matter to court. You must bring all pertinent information with you that has a direct bearing on your case: all receipts for work performed, evidence of phone calls that you had with the repair facility (notes of the calls made, when and by whom), names of the auto repair staff who dealt directly with you, the shop name, your registration, pink slip and any other documents that would serve as evidence in your case. Though going to court is a hassle, it may well be worth the effort to gain damages for personal inconvenience, lost wages and emotional suffering. And we all know that a botched auto repair job or an outright rip-off can have each of those effects on us.

Whatever you decide to do, make sure that you are doing it because you believe it is just or fair. Wild claims of unfair treatment or damages that are not completely accurate can hurt you, especially in an auto repair suit. If there is a countersuit, and you lose, the aggravation can be multiplied. The important thing is for you to realize that you don't have to take it lying down. If you can prove you have been wronged, your chances are excellent that you will recover your damages and maybe a little more to boot!

## CHIN DOWN, GUARD UP

You might be the best haggler in town, or a stickler for detail, but it means nothing if you don't carry the proper attitude.

You should appear dignified, informed, but friendly. You never want to lose one ounce of respect from the start. You can appear to be a fool and set yourself up for fool's ticket if you annoy the staff. So employ a few don'ts.

1. Don't ask shop personnel for a "little brake fluid" or power steering fluid, or "some extra oil," because it is their job to sell you this merchandise. It annoys the hell out of the service manager and/or mechanic. The exception would be if you are paying for other, expensive repairs. If you're having a major brake job done, then asking for a little free brake fluid wouldn't be out of line.

2. Don't ask to borrow tools. A customer who picks up loose tools and begins using them on his car is in for trouble.

3. Don't walk into the shop and stand next to your car. Stand behind the yellow line or ribbon. If there is none, stand outside of the shop doors to watch.

4. Don't approach your car without asking permission or until the mechanic flags you over to look at something. If you do, you'll appear pushy and are liable to aggravate the mechanic or service manager.

5. Don't be unprepared when you make a service visit. Know at least something about the part of your car that is going to be worked on so you can converse with the manager and explain the problem intelligently. If you know absolutely nothing about cars or repair, bring your owner's manual with you and make sure the service manager sees it in your hands. You might nonchalantly place it on the service desk while you are signing the repair invoice. One woman told me that she takes a *Chilton's Motor Manual* with her to the shop, sits in the waiting room, and begins flipping pages when the work is being done on her car. She admits she doesn't know what she's looking at, but the mechanics or service manager don't know that!

# DOING IT YOURSELF

I know of a story where a friend was driving on a freeway when the water temperature gauge suddenly zoomed right up to the danger zone. He immediately shut off the car and coasted to a gas station. He surveyed the engine compartment with the mechanic, and saw that the fan belt had disintegrated. The mechanic also showed him that the water pump had frozen solid. The car could not be driven unless it was repaired. My friend was in a hurry, a point obvious to the mechanic, but was stunned motionless when confronted with a repair estimate of $350! The pump was $100, the fan belt $20 and the rest of the charges were for labor (5 hours @ $39 per hour). When questioned why it cost so much, the mechanic stated the procedure was difficult because he would have to disconnect other items like the air conditioner. My friend, who was not a mechanic, nevertheless knew where the air conditioner was, and saw that it was nowhere near the water pump. When he challenged the mechanic with this, the mechanic looked at him and said, "Hey, do you want to do it yourself?" My friend looked him in the eye and said, "You're damn right I do."

So my friend pushed his car into a vacant lot, called a nearby associate who agreed to lend him a few tools and give him a ride to the nearest parts store. At the store, my friend purchased a rebuilt, generic water pump ($39.95), a fan belt ($6.00) and a *Chilton Repair Manual* for his car ($9.95). He went back to his car, and in full view of the mechanics, changed the water pump and installed the fan belt, filled the radiator with water, then drove right through their gas station honking the horn. Total time: Just under 90 minutes. Total cost: About $60.

Now obviously, my friend in the above example was lucky he had someone to call to lend him some tools. But do you see how much he saved by knowing just the location of some of his parts and by doing it himself? There is no reason why the typical vehicle owner cannot perform some routine repair chores on his car at home. Obviously, some of the major services are outside the reach of the person with limited mechanical ability, i.e., complete valve job service, timing chain replacement, heavy transmission overhaul. However, some of the lighter jobs can be performed quite easily at substantial savings.

## TOOLS

First, go to a parts store or a department store and get a *Chilton* manual for your car. They have a book for nearly every make and model automobile that has ever graced the highways. These manuals include all the service information, specifications and maintenance procedures necessary to repair your car.

Next, get a basic set of tools. Most people have them anyway. This would include a basic socket set, combination open and box end wrenches, two screwdriver sets—Phillips and slot, a plier set, and other numerous pieces. Specialty items, or tools used for specific tasks, like tune-up and brakes, can be found and purchased at reasonable costs. Timing lights, tachometers, vacuum gauges, dwell meters, and compression testers can be found in complete packaged sets that come with handy suitcase containers. Automobile ramps can be bought for as little as $19.95, and you can own your own battery charger for not much more than that. Once you have assembled a good assortment of automotive repair tools you can use them over and over again for the same chores and services. They will pay for themselves quickly.

## TUNE-UP

Substantial savings can be realized quickly with a do-it-yourself minor tune-up. As stated before, the complexity of this service is so overblown that it is known as a "quickie" in the auto repair business. With the newer cars equipped with electronic ignition, the procedure does not amount to more than replacing the spark plugs, distributor cap, rotor, fuel filter and air filter. If you can turn a wrench back and forth, you can do the above, then you can take the car to a mechanic and just ask them to adjust the carburetor, timing or fuel-injection, whatever the case may be.

## OIL & FILTER

If you purchase a set of car ramps, you'll find it possible to get under your car and unscrew the oil pan bolt, let the oil drain, put the bolt back in, remove the oil filter, screw a new one on, then pour in four quarts of high-quality oil that you paid $1 each for. After you do it once or twice, you could do this in about 10 minutes at a cost of about $10.

**Lube**—It is a struggle to lubricate the underneath part of the car's chassis for the average home mechanic. The car really needs to be racked on the proper lift so that leverage and mobility can be used to service the different components and reservoirs. For that, it's best to take the car to a quick stop or gas station.

## BRAKES

Feeling a little adventurous? Ready to take the NIASE exam? A more advanced do-it-yourselfer could accomplish a very good brake job and realize tremendous savings. But the job is very time consuming, and the task must be performed with care and some special tools.

**Pads & Shoes**—You could purchase the necessary brake pads and brake shoes for under $30 in most cases.

**Drums & Rotors**—You can also remove the drums and rotors and take them to a machine shop, or an auto parts store and have them checked and turned. The cost here is generally less than $20. If the drums and rotors are too heavily worn or damaged, the next step would be to go to a junkyard and purchase them in good, used condition, then have them machined. Again, the savings over purchasing new drums and rotors would be tremendous.

## OTHER SIMPLE REPAIRS

Starters and alternators are easily replaced by the home repair person. So are fan belts, fuses, switches, batteries and water, vacuum and fuel hoses. Headlights, taillamps and turn-signal lamps are also easy to repair yourself, often requiring just a Phillips-head screwdriver and the proper part. In some cases, especially with small foreign compacts, the water pump can be changed, like my friend did in the previous example.

If you have an electrical short, pull out your owner's manual and look for the location of your fuse box. Find it and pull out each fuse (there is an inexpensive, special tool to do this) to see if it is okay. An auto fuse can cost pennies, and a confounding electrical problem that could take hours to diagnose, (or set you up for an expensive rip off) may be solved by replacing a blown fuse.

Many people think that if they replace their own headlights they will somehow change the adjustment (the headlight pattern angle). This is not true since headlights are generally secured within their own socket.

By removing the hoop ring retainer—unscrewing three screws, turning the ring and pulling it off—the headlight will exit the socket (as far as its wire harness will allow it). By unsnapping the wire harness the headlight can be taken off and the new one installed. Just remember that the screws in the headlight socket that sit farther back in the seat and have springs behind them are not the headlight mounting screws, but the adjustment screws. You don't want to touch these screws since it would change the headlight adjustment. (Only partially unscrew the mounting screws and this will allow the ring to be rotated and removed.)

## GETTING YOUR OWN PARTS

If a repair shop has to "order out" for a part they've really nothing to do but sit back and wait for a part to be delivered knowing that its markup to the customer is unsolicited profit. Easy money. People can go shopping at a grocery store with discount coupons, and realize the full potential of the savings from packages they have bought. It's different in auto repair. A terrific part found at a parts store does not mean that a repair shop will install it on your vehicle just so you can realize that savings. It is really up to the repair management as to whether they want to or feel like performing such a chore. And that is about as accurate a determining factor that the customer will face.

In most auto repair facilities there is no God-like golden rule that prohibits them from installing out-of-shop or carry-in auto parts on their customers' cars. Not surprisingly, they are very good at making restrictions on the spot, if this happens. The truth is most repair facilities have a flat rate manual or price policy which stipulates how much labor is required for any given part. By logic alone, you would think that if a part comes into their shop it is really no different from one they would supply so why should there be a fuss over installing it per request?

Well, the money factor is one excuse, but also many carry-in parts are just not the correct fitting model replacements; an adapter is missing or some gasket, nut, bolt, shim, or retainer has been left out. And this gives the mechanics headaches when having to scramble around the shop trying to find non-generic parts to custom fit your part to your vehicle. Also, a manager could say that the guarantee/warranty factor would be void if such a part were installed on your vehicle in their shop.

So where does the customer really stand with this carry-his-own-parts-in issue? A little hint: a smaller and slower shop might not frown at this request since they can't afford to turn much work away. Service station mechanics might be a little bit more amiable and understanding, and also not as busy as a large chain. It goes without saying that a sweet smile, a pat on the back and a sugary attitude toward the mechanic or management might dissuade them from turning you down. The worst that could happen is you'd have to take the part back to the parts store for a refund.

Of course the bright spot will occur if you find a repair center that condones this practice. And if you did find one you could certainly realize substantial savings.

---

# WARRANTIES

New car warranties vary from make to make, and their length of coverage depends on the manufacturer. Many people are unaware, however, of the different types of warranties that often come with the purchase of a new car. Knowing exactly how much coverage you have at any given time can help you avoid costly repairs that should have been performed for free.

## TYPES OF WARRANTIES

A *basic warranty* usually covers parts and labor repairs due to defects in materials or workmanship, and it usually includes most of the car except tires and maintenance items. Tires have their own separate warranty offered by the tire manufacturer. Basic warranties vary greatly from carmaker to carmaker, ranging from 1 year/unlimited mileage (Volvo) up to 4 years/50,000 miles (Mercedes-Benz).

*Powertrain warranties* usually start after the basic warranty expires, and offer additional coverage on engine, transmission, U-joints, differential and axles. Some manufacturers, such as Chrysler, offer powertrain warranties for as long as 7 years or 70,000 miles. The average, however, is generally 3 years or 50,000 miles.

A *corrosion warranty* runs concurrently with the basic warranty and offers protection against rust.

An *emissions warranty* is mandated by federal law, requiring that carmakers ensure their cars meet clean air standards for 5 years or 50,000 miles. If your car fails a smog check within this time frame, you should be able to take it back to the dealer and have it repaired free of charge so it'll pass. Emissions warranties cover all areas connected with emissions—including catalytic converters, engine computers and fuel injection systems.

Sometimes, there is a *secret warranty* offered by a manufacturer to cover a repair for a widespread defect in order to avoid a costly and damaging public recall. To protect their market image, manufacturers don't always announce these secret warranties. Ford and Chevrolet offer technical service numbers that are available through dealerships, but to find out if your manufacturer does offer a secret warranty, contact the Center for Auto Safety. For the address, see the sidebar.

Finally, there are *extended service contracts*, which offer additional dealer coverage after the warranty has expired. Do you really need it? Compare the service contract coverage with your warranty and find out how much they really overlap before you decide.

**Voiding Warranties**—A warranty can be void if you use the car for any purpose other than its intended use—such as going off-road, racing, modifying or tampering with emissions equipment. Also, if a tree falls on the car, or it is wiped out by a hurricane, don't look for warranty coverage.

Some warranties are void if you don't perform regular maintenance procedures, such as change the oil. However, you don't necessarily have to have the dealer perform regular maintenance repairs.

A survey by Fram, a manufacturer of oil and air filters, determined that an estimated 1 million new car buyers are told each year that they must have the dealership perform all repairs or the warranty would be void. The truth is, oil, brakes, wipers, headlights and all other simple R & R items can be repaired elsewhere without voiding the original warranty.

**Read Your Warranty**—If you don't ask if your repair is covered under warranty, chances are this information won't be offered. Be sure you study your warranty carefully. Too many people just throw the booklet in the glove compartment where it is soon forgotten. In fact, you should study the warranty *before* you purchase any car. Dealers must provide you with a written warranty upon request prior to the purchase of any car.

# HINT

*The following is a list of agencies you can write to or call if you need help.*

## ARBITRATION PANELS

*Autoline*
*Council of Better Business Bureaus, Inc.*
*1515 Wilson Blvd.*
*Arlington, VA 22209*
*800/228-6505*

*Autocap*
*National Automobile Dealers Association*
*8400 Westpark Dr.*
*McLean, VA 22102*
*703/821-7144*

## LEMON LAWS AND SECRET WARRANTIES

*The Center for Auto Safety*
*2001 S Street N.W., 410*
*Washington, D.C. 20009*
*202/328-7700*

## EMISSIONS WARRANTY INFORMATION

*Director*
*Field Operation and Support Division*
*Environmental Protection Agency*
*401 M Street S.W.*
*Washington, D.C. 20460*

## CALIFORNIA ONLY

*Bureau of Automotive Repair*
*10240 Systems Parkway*
*Sacramento, CA 95827*
*800/952-5210*

# AFTERWORD

Suffice it to say, this is a survival guide. It was written for car owners who are concerned with the astronomical cost of auto repair. It is not a technical repair manual. If that's the type of information you need, then pick up a Chilton, Haynes or Bentley repair manual at your local auto parts store.

My goal was to provide you with enough basic information on what should and what *shouldn't* be done in the most common areas of auto repair. Most certainly, you'll have other repair problems that aren't covered in this book, but hopefully you've gleaned enough general information to deal with a mechanic, service manager or service writer more effectively.

# GLOSSARY

## Parts, terms, and jargon

### Accelerator
The foot pedal which when depressed, opens the throttle valve on the carburetor to allow more engine power and RPM's.

### Acetylene
A colorless gas, C2H2, which when mixed with oxygen is used for welding metals. It can be seen in most shops contained in a portable rack on wheels that has two cylinders.

### Additives
Extra prescription, liquefied chemicals that are added to the car's oil, gas, radiator, and transmission reservoir. Their design is to enhance or modify the standard liquids and lubricants. Friction proofing oil additives and anti-freeze are examples.

### Alignment
The process by which a mechanic sets the front suspension parts of your car to factory specifications. Three adjustments are commonly made: toe, camber, and caster.

### Alternator
The device that has replaced the older generator, used for the purpose of supplying recharging current to the battery when the engine is running, and supplying current to operate the vehicle's electrical equipment.

### Ammeter
An ammeter is an instrument that measures the amount of electricity in amperes being charged into or discharged from the car's battery.

### Ampere
A unit of electricity, based on the amount of electrical current sent by one volt through a basic resistance unit called an ohm.

### Anchor Block
Also known as stars or self adjusters, these are the small parts that expand the rear brake shoes during adjustment. Self-adjusting brakes seldom work right and must be manually adjusted. If a mechanic tells you that you need new anchor blocks, just tell him to disassemble the ones you have and clean them. It should be part of the brake service and is easily done.

## Arcing

Involves chamfering brakes shoes on a brake lathe in order to fit them exactly to the inside profile of a brake drum. It is a process that is necessary to achieve 100% braking efficiency, yet it is almost always left out of a standard brake job, or it is seldom done right by a mechanic.

## Armature

An iron core wound with wire. It is the revolving part of an electric motor or alternator.

## Asbestos

A fire and heat-resistant fabric or material which is used to insulate electrical components or serve as a protective heat barrier or shield. Brake shoes and pads have asbestos properties to protect them from heat.

## Axle

The shaft on which the wheels of an automobile turn.

## Back Flush Machine

A machine that uses pressure and valves to flush the radiator, cooling system, and heater core of a vehicle in any and all directions of flow. It is designed specifically for this function and no other. It is really the only way to rid a cooling system of all rust, debris and oil coolant.

## Bald

A term used to describe worn-out tires.

## Ball Bearing, or Bearing

Encased, freely rolling metal balls or needle pins designed to carry the weight and torque of a revolving shaft or wheel.

## Ball Joint

A front-end part that supports the car's chassis. It works on a ball and socket principle and must be lubed regularly. It receives more stress than upper ball joints and is replaced more often. An alignment usually follows lower ball joint replacement.

## Belted (tires)

Tires are made from different materials and constructed for certain purposes. Belted, bias-belted, and radial designs are commonplace. Tires can have fiberglass or steel belts in their construction.

## Better Business Bureau (BBB)

An agency that can help you with an auto repair suit or claim. They can examine the current records of any repair business and find out how reputable they are; what their track record is for ethical behavior and customer satisfaction. A good place to take a complaint.

## Big Ten

This is a term that I use to refer to the most common areas of R & R, or fast auto repair. It is a general list in which I include: front end work, tune-up, brakes, tires, batteries, starters and alternators, exhaust, alignment, smog checks, the L.O.F service, and the transmission service (fluid change). Air conditioning service (evacuation and recharge) can be considered to be on the outside of this major listing, as is water pump and cooling system work. Other areas of repair are certainly done by most shops and many of the other repairs are interrelated to the big ten. Wheel bearing and axle seal and bearing replacement are related to brakes or front end.

## Bureau of Automotive Repair (BAR)

This is a state regulated authority in California that monitors and approves licenses and education of mechanics. It is also a source for the consumer who has a repair complaint who wishes to levy charges against a repair facility. The BAR can be contacted by phone (their numbers are listed in plain view in most shops), and a counselor can set up an appointment for the purpose of intervention or litigation. California customers who have been ripped off are advised to contact the BAR office nearest them.

## Bleed (Brakes)

This is a term used to describe the elimination of old brake fluid from a car's hydraulic brake system, or the ridding of air in the brake lines. A power bleed is preferred over a manual one.

## Block

The main body of the engine. The central casting around which the rest of the engine is built and bolted on.

## Blow-by

Usually typical of a worn-out or older engine. It is the condition where oil "blows by" the piston rings and into the combustion chamber. Blue smoke emitting from the exhaust and oil-fouled plugs are the result. The solution is to rebuild the engine and replace the piston rings—a major expense.

## Bonus or Bonus Shop

This is a condition in which a repair shop sponsors a bonus or commission program. The more parts and services a mechanic sells the more money he gets as compensation for his salesmanship. This means he is motivated to sell as many unneeded parts and services as he can. Avoid all bonus or commission shops. These types of work programs are destructive and cost the consumer untold misery and financial loss.

## Boot

The rubber cup or retainer used to encase and protect front end parts like the tie-rod ends and ball joints.

## Bore

The inside diameter of a cylinder. Cylinder bore and wheel cylinder bore are examples.

## Brake Pad

A device squeezed onto a rotating disc to slow or stop your car. It is used on disc brakes.

## Brake Shoe

The curved metal arc upon which the brake lining material is riveted or glued. It is used on drum brakes.

## Bushing

A replaceable metal, rubber, or other fiber material used to protect that part which it supports. It reduces friction and can absorb shock. Upper control arm bushing and transmission pilot bushing, are examples.

## Cam

A protrusion on a shaft or wheel which imparts an eccentric, or irregular motion to provide a specific or timed energy for another part or system. Distributor cam and camshaft are two such devices.

## Camping Out—Vacationing—Pitching a Tent

All terms that refer to a mechanic who is taking forever on a repair job, usually because he's stuck or doesn't know what he is doing. If a mechanic cannot get the car back to its owner at the appointed time he tells the manager that "it's spending the night." The manager in turn has to call up the owner and inform him that "we've got to keep her overnight."

## Carb (Carburetor)

The mixing component found on some cars with internal combustion engines. It mixes or atomizes in correct proportions the raw fuel and air that is induced into the engine for the purpose of combustion.

## Catalytic Converter

The catalytic converter (sometimes referred to as a CAT) is a metal canister that is part of the emission control system. It functions as an afterburner by using chemicals and very high temperatures to burn off excess hydrocarbons and carbon monoxide. It is nearly indestructible and many claims of its vulnerability are imagined and deceiving. If a mechanic tells you it needs to be replaced, go to the dealership. First of all, CATS rarely go bad, but if they do, their replacement is usually covered by a federally mandated warranty.

## Charge

The restoration of electricity to a car's battery by supplying slow and steady current over a period of time. Or, an outrageous amount of money you are requested to pay for what seems like simple work.

## Carry-In

It is a part that you bring into a shop for the purpose of installation. Some shops have strict rules about installing outside source parts that they do not order themselves. It takes a great deal of diplomacy and sweet talk to get this favor. Good luck.

## Chassis

The lower frame, wheels and underbody of a motor vehicle.

## Choke

A valve or flap located in the top of the carburetor used for the purpose of cutting off incoming air. This action, when initiated, richens the fuel mixture for cold-starting and warm-up.

## Combi Kit

The package of hardware that is used to keep brake parts in place, such as the keepers and return springs.

## Come-Back

This is a customer who takes his car back to an auto repair shop because it was not repaired correctly. The number of come-backs a mechanic gets usually denotes how inept he is at troubleshooting and repair.

## Condenser

A device for receiving or holding a charge of electricity. The most common condenser can be found in the distributor cap in cars that have standard ignition. It absorbs electricity and feeds it out in correct amounts to the spark plugs.

## Core (Core part)

A core can be that inner part of a larger working component, such as a radiator core, or a heater core (the main container in this case). A core part is a part that is usually reserviceable or rebuildable. Starters, alternators, water pump, carburetors, and some tires and batteries have core value to repair shops. Core parts are sold to machine shops or specialty repair houses so they can be rebuilt or remanufactured using new inner components. They can then be sold back to repair shops as "rebuilts."

## Cotter Pin

A fastening device used to hold machinery or linkage together. Many are found on carburetor linkages and front end parts.

## Cowl

A metal housing which supports a larger part or structure. An engine or radiator cowl is used to direct the flow of air to a specific area.

## Crankcase

The metal container in which the engine's crankshaft is located.

## Cubes or Cubic inch

Usually denotes engine capacity. It is the area expressed in cubic inches contained in the total number of cylinders that your car contains. Thus, if you have a 320 cubic-inch engine, and that engine has eight cylinders, each cylinder has 40 cubic inches. The more cubic inches, the larger the cylinder and overall cubic-inch displacement. Many foreign make cars express this measurement in cc's, which stands for cubic centimeter.

## CV Joint

The constant velocity joint of a car that has front-wheel drive. It transmits the power from the engine to a shaft that drives the front wheel. Also known as a constant velocity joint.

## Dealership

The car manufacturer's outlet for both new and used car sales and auto repair. Ford, Chrysler, and Toyota are examples.

## Diameter

A straight line or measurement between the two opposing or furthest points of a round cylinder or shaft. The inside part of a brake drum has a diameter measured in inches.

## Diesel

A vehicle that has a diesel engine and is designed to run on diesel fuel only. Diesel engines are normally more heavily constructed and durable than other engines.

## Differential Gear (rear end, third member)

It is the rear section of the car that receives transmitted power from the engine and driveline. It is a train of gears designed to permit two or more shafts to revolve at different speeds. Typically, the ring gear, driveshaft gear, and pinion gear are located in the differential housing.

## Disc Brakes

The most efficient brakes devised today. They are large metal discs mounted on axles inside the wheels. The brake is activated when two brake pads are compressed against the disc.

## Distributor

The device used to send quick bursts of electricity to the spark plugs at precise time intervals by use of a condenser, points or vane, rotor, and distributor cap.

## Dynamometer or "Dyno"

This is an electrically operated machine which measures the torque and horsepower of a car at the rear wheels. The rear wheels are placed on rollers so they can rotate at different speeds, transmitting data to the dynamometer. It can be used to isolate a bad plug, points, coil, or other electrical malfunction while under true driving load.

## Duct

These are tubes, hoses, or pipes which direct airflow, mostly. You can have a heater duct, a defroster duct, or a muffler tailpipe duct. You can see them under the dashboard, those accordion-like fabric hoses that route air to vents.

## Electronic Ignition

The new improved ignition system currently installed on new cars. It has fewer moving parts than the older standard ignition, requires less maintenance, and lasts much longer.

## Evacuation/Recharge

This means to draw out old freon gas out of an air conditioning system and recharge or supply it with new gas.

## Factory Part

A part that carries the name of its manufacturer. It can be expressed, Original Ford Factory Part. The general hype associated with factory parts is that they are somehow superior to all others. This is not always the case. There are many quality parts that are exact and even better reproductions than the original.

## Fan

An impeller or vane used to circulate, force, or drive air to a certain area or over a device. Most fans are used for cooling purposes, such as a radiator fan.

## Farmed Out

This is a service that must be bought outside the facility. This drives the cost of the service up.

## Fender

The outside skirt or portion of a car that covers a wheel opening. Also called a wheel arch.

## Final Cut

A brake drum or rotor is cut or resurfaced on a brake lathe. The initial cut is the rough or first cut. The second or finishing mode is the fine cut. Tragically, the fine cut is being left out nowadays by impatient mechanics who want to rush the job instead, because the final cut takes twice as long as the rough cut.

## Flat Rate

A flat rate manual (shop book) lists the different labor times required to do a specific repair job on a vehicle. Most dealerships carry a flat rate manual that has fixed labor times. Tire shops, department stores, and other repair facilities might have their own company flat rate book so the prices do vary from one facility to another. An expression 1.5 hrs means that the job will take one and one half hours to complete. If the shop flat rate is $60.00 per hour, the cost will be $90.00.

## Friction

The resistance of one moving surface against another, which when extreme and non-lubricated, produces heat and wear. Engine parts wear due to friction when they come in constant contact with each other.

## Front End

This refers to the undercarriage parts of your car that deal with steering and suspension. Ball joints, control arm bushings, tie rods, and strut rod bushings are front end parts. Alignment is also referred to as front end work.

## Fuel Injection

Fuel is injected directly into the intake port of a combustion chamber by this system, which is computer controlled. It is an improvement over the older carburetor system which does not compensate for changes in vacuum, pressure change, and load factors the way fuel injection is designed to do. Better gas mileage and performance can be attributed to fuel injection.

## Fuse Block

This is the container that holds the various accessory fuses for your car. It is generally located under the dashboard or in the engine compartment.

## Fuse

This is a small protection device designed to blow or break its connection when it receives a higher than normal current load. They are allocated to protect individual accessory circuits like the radio or windshield wipers. They are readily replaced and very cheap in cost.

## Gasket

A material or object used to seal opposing metal or other surfaces when they are sandwiched together. Gaskets prevents leaks and contain pressure. A head gasket forms a leak-proof seal between the cylinder head and the engine block.

## Gears

These are wheels with teeth that mesh with other wheels with teeth or splines. They connect one driving force to another. One gear can change the speed of another by its size and number of teeth.

## General Manager

He's the big boss at a dealership. The general manager, who may not know much about auto repair, still has authority over the service manager. A dispute that cannot be handled by you and the service manager can be taken to the general manager. Most service managers fear the power of this higher-up. Surprisingly, general managers will take the side of the customer in many cases, and dress down the service manager for being inept at handling customer satisfaction. If all else fails, scream for the General!

## Hanger

An exhaust mounting bracket that might include a fabric or rubber shock band or coupler.

## Heavy Duty

Batteries and shocks commonly carry this connotation, and it can be a gross exaggeration at times. Simply, it means that a heavy-duty replacement part has been devised and manufactured that surpasses the originally designed factory part in some way. They claim that the heavy-duty part is bigger, stronger, and lasts longer. It is mostly a sales or promotion gimmick with a little truth.

## Hood-Up Syndrome

If a mechanic has finished working on your car early, and he knows that you are waiting for it, he will prop the hood and leave the fender covers on your car to disguise the fact that he finished early with it. He does this because he knows that you might know what the flat rate labor time is on the car. If you question him why your car has been deserted for so long he might tell you that he was waiting for a part. However, he has actually been out of sight from you working on his next car and waiting for the flat rate labor time to expire before he releases your car.

## Horsepower

This is a general, archaic term used to define the basic strength, power, or speed of a car. Technically, it is a foot-pound-second unit of power, equal to 550 foot-pound per second. This term has been used to commercial success in advertising domestic automobiles. It can be measured at the driveshaft, or rear wheels. Another reliable and easier source to measure power is, acceleration from a dead stop and peak acceleration. Horsepower alone is not a logical indicator of a car's true performance capabilities.

## Hydrometer

An instrument used to measure the specific gravity of a liquid. Battery water (acid) is measured this way.

## Hydraulic

A motor or machinery that is assisted by or operated by the applied pressure of a liquid, as in hydraulic brakes.

## Ignition

It is the series of all electrical components and systems that contribute to the eventual firing of the spark plugs. It involves the primary and secondary circuits. Ignition is also the process by which combustion takes place in the cylinders. The fuel/air mixture "ignites" in the cylinder producing power. Not to be confused with the car's ignition switch key.

## In-House

A term used to define a shop that does its own specialty work, like precision machine shop work, or radiator recoring.

## Installer

A low grade R & R mechanic. Muffler mechanics are actually installers. They are not diagnosticians.

## Journeyman

This was a term that used to apply to mechanics who were undergoing an apprenticeship program in a repair shop. The required time period was usually two to five years before the apprentice was promoted to a a journeyman position. This term has lost its meaning simply because anyone now can call themselves a journeyman who has been on the job for awhile. It takes no study, license or certificate to be recognized as a journeyman. It is much more relevant in other crafts and trades such as plumbers and air conditioning/heating technicians. It was adopted and misused by the auto industry.

## L.O.F.
The initials for lube, oil, and filter. This is a package service, one of the most commonly performed at all repair shops.

## Lot Lizard (Detailer, lot boy)
Usually low man on the totem pole at a dealership. If a mechanic stains your car's interior, it's a fair bet that the lot lizard will have to clean it.

## Low Speed Adjustment
Performed during a smog certification, this adjustment is made when your car fails a smog check. It usually involves nothing more than a timing or carburetor adjustment, but costs around $25 extra. It is made to bring your car into allowable specification for the emission of excessive hydrocarbons or carbon monoxide. The test machine actually makes the determination and the mechanic makes the physical adjustment to correct it.

## Manifold
The device used to route burned exhaust from the cylinders to the exhaust pipe.

## Master
This could be the master brake cylinder that is located in your engine compartment and holds a reservoir of brake fluid. Or it could be the title to a technician who has passed all eight of the required repair tests set forth by the National Institute for Automotive Service Excellence. The Master Mechanic is the most proficient and educated craftsman.

## Matching Wrenches
This means that two high-powered mechanics are competing against each other. It is a machismo display that happens in all shops; one mechanic tries to out-bonus the other by replacing more parts and performing more services. It's all ego, akin to "king of the hill." However, it is devastating to a customer because work gets rushed and over-sold to the general public. Just about all shops function like this—the need for each mechanic to make his "kill" or ticket bigger by the end of the week.

## Mechanic
A general name given to someone who works on some part of a car. A tire buster can call himself a mechanic. An R & R mechanic is really an assembler or installer of parts.

## Mic

Mic is short for micrometer, a tool used to measure the inside diameter of a cylinder or sphere. The measurement is expressed in thousandths of an inch. If a mechanic tells you that your brakes drums didn't "mic" out, he means that the drum diameter was too large to permit resurfacing. An outside micrometer is used to measure the thickness of brake rotors and the same rule applies for a given allowable thickness, set forth by the manufacturer.

## Miss

The misfiring of a cylinder as a result of a failed component like a plug, plug wire, or carburetor problem.

## Muffler

The canister device located under the car's chassis that suppresses noise and arrests spark. Some mufflers contain deadening materials like fiberglass and asbestos.

## N/C (No Charge)

You might see this written on your repair receipt after you have had an inspection on your car. It means that they have charged you nothing to troubleshoot your car's problem. A brake inspection is often free at department and chain store repair shops, as are other inspections. However, this is about the only time you'll ever see this on an auto repair invoice.

## NIASE (National Institute for Automotive Service Excellence)

This is the most widely respected training and certification program for mechanics who wish to be licensed and certified in the various areas of automotive repair, body and paint work. It is strictly a voluntary program and does cost money for registration and the course. But any mechanic or technician wearing the "blue seal of excellence" should be regarded as the best in the industry. The mechanic who passes all eight areas of repair is designated as a "master" in the trade. He would be equivalent to a four-year term college automotive engineer, only he is actually "on-line" and performing the physical work.

## Octane

This is really an additive given to gasoline that has an anti-knock quality. It cuts down on ping or knock. It has very little to do with producing "more power." The higher the octane rating, the more anti-knock serum it has.

## Official Station

This can be an official brake repair, smog, or head lamp adjusting station. They can be recognized by large state signs displayed on the facade of the shop or affixed near it. After a court decision (as a result of an equipment violation given by a traffic officer) that requires you to repair one of these items, you are designated to have it done at one of these officially recognized stations to show proof that a legal entity has confirmed the proper repair.

## On The Hook

This is a car that has been towed back to a repair shop that did not properly fix the car's problem. It is the ultimate nightmare of the service manager and mechanic. Mechanics lose face when their car comes back on the hook. This is the most irritating position in which a customer can be. It can also be time for legal action.

## Overhaul

The complete rebuilding of an engine using major engine components; pistons, rods, bearings, valves, etc.

## Owner's Manual

The booklet that comes with your car. It contains all the information you need for light repair, service and vehicle operation. It also has diagrams and charts. Almost no one ever reads it, but I think you should start. It's never too late, right?

## Piston

The piston is a cylindrical part that rides up and down in the cylinder shaft. It is compressed or driven downward by the explosion of ignited fuel, then continues a cycle, driving upward to force spent exhaust out of the chamber into the exhaust manifold. It is fitted with rings, usually three, that make a tight seal between it and the cylinder wall. If your car has four cylinders, it has four pistons, one for each cylinder.

## Points

The small pair of contacts located inside the distributor. They open and close via the rotation of the distributor cam to provide spark at a given interval which fires a spark plug.

## Power Bleed

A method of bleeding or ridding the brake system of a car of air and old brake fluid. It involves the use of a pressurized tank, fittings and hose. It is considered to be the modern way of bleeding brakes as opposed to the old manual method, where two mechanics are used, one to pump up the brake pedal, and the other who must bleed off a valve. Power bleeding is a one step, clean and swift process performed by only one mechanic.

## Prorated

Sometimes a tire shop will prorate, or give you credit on a new set of tires if you have an old set of their tires with which you are dissatisfied with, or that have failed prematurely due to inferior workmanship. A prorate guarantee gives you a discount sometimes if you were responsible for wearing out the tires before their warranty/guarantee deadline.

## Quick Stop

Usually a drive-in type repair shop that promises quick and fast service and repair. They are the smallest shops in the industry, frequently located in gutted service stations. Their claim of "service while you wait" is exaggerated and their working habits are usually rushed and substandard.

## Rack

Also called a lift. It is the mechanical device used to hoist your car in the air so a mechanic can work under it. A pit is a hole in the floor so a car can be pulled over it allowing a mechanic to work underneath it.

## Radiator

The radiator is a cooling device mostly located at the front of a vehicle to catch onrushing air for the purpose of cooling. The radiator fan also helps to suck or draw outside air against the radiator body. It contains multiple inside shells or passages which are designed to dissipate heat quickly. Many are made of copper construction.

## Rag Wrench

An inexperienced mechanic. One who is even below the status of an apprentice.

## Rebuilt

A term applied to a core part like an alternator, water pump, or starter that can be refurbished with the addition of new parts. Rebuilt parts are of lesser quality than new parts. Rarely do they last as long or carry full protection warranty/guarantees.

## Recap

An old tire that has received a retread of new rubber. It is more common to recap large truck tires than car tires, and it is generally advised not to buy recaps because of their rapid failure rate and substandard guarantees.

## Repair Order

Also known as the invoice or repair bill, it is your paperwork or receipt itemizing the labor and parts costs. The guarantee or warranty might also be written on the Repair Order.

## Rotation
Tires are rotated on a car to provide even wear distribution. Owner's manuals have the correct sequence for rotating the tires to different axles. A "five tire" rotation includes the spare tire.

## R & R
These are initials for remove and replace. For instance, a muffler is a common and quickly replaced R & R part. A mechanic who replaces just mufflers is an R & R type mechanic. There is little creativity or diagnostic thinking when replacing such parts. The process is routine. A dealership technician must actually think and reason in many cases when he is working on a complicated system that needs problem-solving talents. A dealership technician, generally, is not referred to as an R & R mechanic. He is a true technician.

## Scare Tactics
These are phrases that are designed to frighten the customer into making a part or service purchase. The phrases usually involve a topic related to safety and they are intended to attack the customer's con-science and well being.

## Seal Beam
This is the technical term for a headlight lamp.

## Service Manager
Sometimes called the service writer, he is the individual with whom the repair customer deals with pertaining to the actual repair and cost. He is the middleman and salesman between you and the mechanic or technician.

## Sham
A device used to deceive the public by making an untrue claim or by falsifying a diagnosis. Scam is the same thing—a rip-off.

## Shock Absorbers
The tubes or cartridges located underneath and near the four corners of the car. They absorb the up and down jolts and jars of the chassis by dampening the coil spring action. The coil or leaf spring actually takes the road shock, but it is the shock absorber that halts the momentum produced by the spring.

## Short
Another word for an electrical malfunction in a circuit, motor or wiring harness.

## Smog Check

A procedure for taking your car into an official repair station for the purpose of state-required smog certification. In California, you must take your car in every two years for certification to make sure it complies with current pollutant and emission control standards. The smog check program was instituted to clean up the environment by finding and prosecuting "gross violators," cars emitting excessive and intolerable amounts of exhaust pollutants.

## Sniffer

Mechanics jargon for the exhaust gas probe that is inserted into the tailpipe of a vehicle for the purpose of testing emission control gases.

## Solenoid

The solenoid is a switching device that is part of the car's ignition or starting system. By turning the key you send current from the battery to the solenoid. This trips a magnet and pulls the starter motor's contacts together so that the starter motor is activated. Its primary function is a heavy-duty switch device or relay.

## Specialty Shop

Usually a satellite or spinoff from a foreign car dealership, these privately owned repair shops can be a real gem since they offer dealership quality work and prices at reduced costs on a specific make of car. They are an excellent alternative to the higher costing dealership.

## Suspension

Suspension is the collection of all springs, leverage devices, support frames, and undercarriage parts that support the weight of the vehicle.

## Technician

The present term identifying a mechanic. It is an overrated, or flowery connotation used by most repair facilities to label their mechanics in a more professional sense. The only people deserving of such a term would be automotive engineers, licensed and certified dealership mechanics, or "Master" mechanics. There is nothing technical about a tire buster.

## Thermostat

A device used in the car's cooling system to stabilize the temperature of the circulating water. For starting purposes the thermostat remains closed to restrict the circulation of water, thus assisting to warm the engine. When sufficient operating temperature is reached, the thermostat opens to allow the flow of cooling water to the engine head and block. Thermostats have temperature ratings measured in degrees Fahrenheit.

## Tie Rods
The rods and linkages that connect your steering mechanism with your front wheels. Tie rod ends are the knuckle-type joints that join one rod to another.

## Torque
This is a term used to identify twisting or turning force put out by a driving shaft and transmitted to another mechanical device. The less resistance a turning shaft has against another element, the more torque it has.

## Transmission
A housed system of gears and mechanisms that transmits the power output of your engine to the wheels in gradual and controlled amounts. In an automatic transmission, torque from the engine is shifted by different gears to enable smooth and increased speed.

## Transmission Service
Not to be confused with transmission repair, this is a fluid, gasket and filter change for the automatic transmission. Nearly all types of shops perform this service. A repair involves taking the transmission apart, which should only be done by a dealership or specialty shop.

## Troubleshooting
The means by which a mechanic searches down a mechanical fault, usually achieved by the process of elimination.

## Tune-Up
A procedure or service involved with accomplishing peak performance and fuel economy by working on and replacing certain ignition parts on an engine. This includes the replacement of spark plugs, wires, points and fine-tuning adjustments on the carburetor or fuel injection system. Major and minor tune-ups are distinctions between a complicated, or more thorough, tune-up and that of the standard or ordinary type.

## U-joint or Universal Joint
A coupling device of the driveshaft to the differential gear at the rear axle. It permits an off-angle joining of the driveshaft and the rear end.

## Zerk
This is a nipple-shaped grease fitting connected to a front end part for the purpose of lubrication.

# INDEX

Shams and scams. *See also* Scare
   tactics
   Arbitration panels, 173
   Better Business Bureau, 165
   Bureau of Automotive Repair, 165
   exhaust systems/mufflers, 76-79
   secret warranties, 171
   small claims court, 165-166
   smog checks, 158-160
   tune-ups, 144-149
   what to do, 163-166, 173
Shock absorbers, 9, 13, 17, 107-110
Smog check, 13, 21, 22, 153-161
   analysis, 155-157
   cost, 157
   emission control function, 154
   initial inspection, 154-155
   passing, 157
   recertification, 157-158
   retest, 157
   shams, 158-160
Solenoid, 126
Spark plugs, 136-138
   heat range, 136-137
   inspection, 137-138
   wear, 136
   wires, 139-140
Specialty shops, 22-24
   best for repairs of, 24
   costs, 23
   mechanics, 35-36
Springs, 13
Starter, 123-127
   diagnosing problems, 124-127
   do-it-yourself, 169
   new vs. rebuilt, 126-127
   solenoid, 126
   what mechanic should do, 126
Steering, 13
Suspension, 13

**T**
Taillights, 10, 20, 169
Tailpipe, 18
Tie rod ends, 17, 55, 103-104
Timing, 141
Tires, 8, 10, 13, 17, 58-63
   balancing, 61-62
   brand names, 58
   inflation, 59
   inner tubes, I0
   inspection, 58
   mixing, 60-61
   pressure gauge, 59
   replacement, 60-62

   rotation, 59-60
   scare tactics, 62-63
   tire stores, 17
   tread indicators, 58
   valve stems, 62
   warranty/guarantee, 62
Toe, 65-66
Tools, 167-168
Transmission, 9, 13
   fluid, 21, 57
   service, 22
Tune-up, 9, 17, 21, 22, 133-151
   adjustments, 141
   air filter, 141, 148
   basic, 13
   checklist, 148
   distributor, 138-139
   do-it-yourself, 168
   electronic, 143
   fuel filter, 140-141
   fuel injection, 144
   idle speed, 141
   ignition, 135
   major, 135-142
   minor, 19
   PCV valve, 140
   shams, 144-149
   spark plugs, 136-138
   spark plug wires, 139-140
   timing, 141
   what mechanic should do, 142
   when to get, 134-135

**U**
Universal joints, 55, 100

**V**
Vacuum system, 20
Valve stems, 62

**W**
Warranties, 171-172
   basic, 171
   corrosion, 171
   emissions, 171
   powertrain, 171
   secret, 171
   warranty work, 12
Water pump, 9-10, 20, 169
Wheel bearings, 17, 100
Wheels, 13
Windshield wipers, 10, 20, 57